DRINK *like a* LOCAL

NEW ORLEANS

A Field Guide to
New Orleans' Best Bars

Drink Like a Local: New Orleans
A Field Guide to New Orleans' Best Bars

13-Digit ISBN: 978-1-64643-423-7
10-Digit ISBN: 1-64643-423-4

This book may be ordered by mail from the publisher. Please include $5.99 for postage and handling. Please support your local bookseller first!

Books published by Cider Mill Press Book Publishers are available at special discounts for bulk purchases in the United States by corporations, institutions, and other organizations. For more information, please contact the publisher.

Cider Mill Press Book Publishers
"Where good books are ready for press"
501 Nelson Place
Nashville, Tennessee 37214

cidermillpress.com

Typography: Ballinger, Condor, Pacifico, Poppins, Stolzl

Printed in Malaysia

23 24 25 26 27 OFF 5 4 3 2 1
First Edition

DRINK *like a* LOCAL
NEW ORLEANS

*A Field Guide to
New Orleans' Best Bars*

CAMILLE WHITWORTH
& SIDNEY WEBB

CIDER MILL PRESS

BOOK PUBLISHERS

CONTENTS

Baybeh...this is New Orleans, where cocktails are a major part of our culture. It's a place where there is always something to drink for anyone who is thirsty. There are so many places to discover and explore because, after all, there is always a story at the bottom of every glass. It takes a champion to fully explore what is said to be one of the world's most whimsical playgrounds for cocktail lovers in a city where many classics are believed to have been created. History tells us that the first cocktail created in America was invented here. The Sazerac dates back to the mid-1800s. Our historic bars, creative bartenders, and those who sit on barstools across the Crescent City may all agree, New Orleans is the foundation of civilized drinking.

To drink like a local takes many twists and turns in New Orleans. While we love our longstanding historic places, we also support dive bars, mom-and-pops, and trendy haunts. The common denominator in every bar here is comfort and diversity...otherwise, you may struggle with success. The magic of our community lies in coming together, whether it be for food, music, or drinks, where we like to meet new friends and keep good company.

There are many popular bars on visitors' lists of "must-go-to places" that locals frequent as well, so they don't feel like tourist traps. New Orleans is a place that sparks romance, curiosity, spontaneity, and revelry. It seems most everyone has a story of their visit to the Big Easy. It's a place where you can let your hair down and no one will blink an eye. In fact, don't be surprised if you get an approving nod or a thumbs up for just being yourself, without inhibitions. You may be invited to take part in some of our unconventional events, like the annual Red Dress Run, where even men wear their best red gowns and heels, or the World Naked Bike Ride, or the Running of the Bulls, where ladies on Rollerblades chase you down with plastic bats... for fun.

Coming here fuels inspiration deep in your spirit, with the many artists, street performers, second line parades, musicians, and, yes, the cocktail culture. Our most seasoned bartenders are solid on making the classics, and they work with excitement to preserve the era of past cocktails while creating new trends.

I've never heard anyone get on a plane and say, "I'm going to New Orleans, and I'm going to stay sober." Ha! Even programs like Tales of the Cocktail originated here, which draws cocktail people of all kinds from around the world. Its weeklong annual event puts a spotlight on top bartenders, cocktail lovers, distillers, and educators. All who come share their experience and passion for the industry.

Simply put, New Orleanians are serious about their bars, drinks, and those who make them. We all have a favorite spot. The COVID-19 pandemic forced many of those watering holes to close, the ultimate final last call. For those of us who made it through, we are high on the excitement that the history of drinking hasn't come to an end and, as far as we can see, it won't halt anytime soon.

In *Drink like a Local: New Orleans*, we break it all down, from our sacred dive bars to fun pubs and breweries, from cheerful cocktail lounges to popular watering holes. So, as we say here in the Crescent City, "*Laissez les bon temps rouler*" ("let the good times roll,") and make sure you always have a good drink in hand. Cheers!

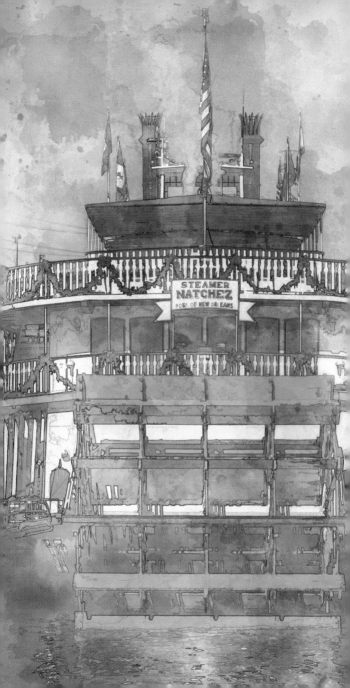

FRENCH QUARTER

This small historic neighborhood is mainly famous for live jazz music and the feel of old-school speakeasies. Strolling the streets or dancing in them will be best done with a glass of champagne, a frozen daiquiri or a classic Sazerac.

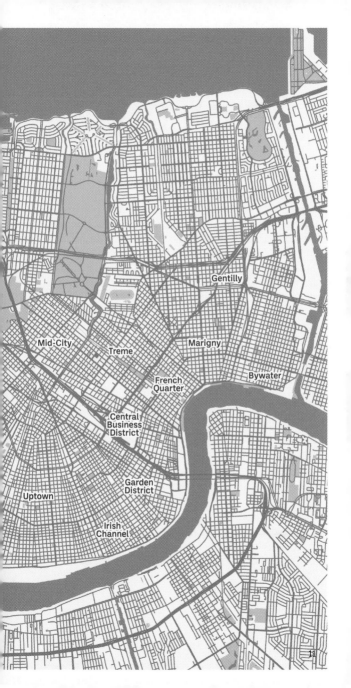

Mid-City

Treme

Gentilly

Marigny

Bywater

French
Quarter

Central
Business
District

Uptown

Garden
District

Irish
Channel

ERIN ROSE

811 Conti Street
New Orleans, LA 70112

The Erin Rose motto is "Local Chaos, Local Prices, Local Love." Enough said, right? Step inside, and you instantly feel the popularity of the place. Its two rooms are usually completely packed with regulars, who range from local celebrities, writers, musicians, and well-behaved dogs to curious visitors.

This cozy neighborhood Irish pub with great drinks holds a heck of a lot of history. Formerly a private home, its old brick fireplace is still visible. The house was turned into a bar in the 1950s and has been serving ever since.

The eclectic décor—the walls are covered with photos, neon signs, old musical instruments, stickers, fun quotes, and many more artifacts—beckons through the windows, whose shutters are always open, rain or shine. It's a vibe that reminds you of a house museum of sorts. There's even an old cigarette machine that still works!

Just steps away from the famed Bourbon Street, this hidden gem is where locals and visitors come to escape, especially late at night. Most famous for its Frozen Irish Coffee and affordable drinks, if you ask the bartenders for the second-best thing on the menu, they're likely to offer you a shot of vodka.

JEWEL OF THE SOUTH

1026 St. Louis Street
New Orleans, LA 70112

For centuries we have been known as the city that drinks morning, noon, and night, both personally and professionally. So it's only fitting that we end up inside the 1830s nouveau-chic Jewel of the South, where their modern drink menu is refreshingly fun, a bit advanced, intentional, and symbolic of the fresh, hip cocktail scene led by New Orleans' most notable bartenders, including cocktail trailblazer and James Beard award winner Chris Hannah, who is serving up some serious drinks here. The two-story building is warmly decorated with nineteenth-century flair and reeks of sweet Southern charm, which puts most any busy mind at ease as soon as they walk through the door.

This is one of the city's top drinking spots, to be sure. Ask for Chris; he's traveled the world spreading wisdom and learning tricks of the cocktail trade. During Mardi Gras, try his Cajun Bon Vivant, which includes the juices from pork fat and is served with a large ice cube that has a king cake baby frozen inside. I tell you, it's altogether delicious.

If you love hospitality and feeling good, then come on over to a place that reminds you of home. In fact, this Creole cottage was a family home until a few years ago, when it was transformed. The patio looks like something out of a Tuscan vineyard. The bar is small, but in a nice way that allows you to spend intimate time with the bartender or the person sitting next to you.

THE NIGHT TRIPPER

1¾ oz. bourbon

¾ oz. amaro

¼ oz. Liquore Strega

2 dashes Peychaud's Bitters

Orange twist, to garnish

1. Stir all ingredients into mixing glass with ice.
2. Strain over ice into an old fashioned glass.
3. Garnish with the orange twist.

ARNAUD'S FRENCH 75 BAR

813 Rue Bienville
New Orleans, LA 70112

Most classic cocktails are associated with a whole lot of mystery about where they came from. The French 75 goes all the way back to 1915, and a visit to its namesake bar is always a history lesson. The bar started out as an all-male dining room annex of the highly popular Arnaud's Restaurant, with highbrow French décor and impeccably dressed drinkers.

Many of the bartenders have been here for years and love talking about the various cocktails they've invented along the way. They wear tuxedos, which puts a well-deserved exclamation point on the sense of passion poured into most glasses. You can obviously get the classics as well as modern creations and, of course, the signature French 75, a blend of cognac and champagne. It doesn't hurt that in 2019 the bar, with then-head bartender Chris Hannah, won the James Beard Award for Outstanding Bar Program.

Quick history: The drink got its name because it was believed back then that the original combination of ingredients was so powerful, it mimicked the impact of the light and powerful French 75 guns used in World War I. Pow!

Most drinks here are derived from French culture, sophisticated and stiff, and enjoyed by high-end clientele celebrating a special occasion or a group wrapping up a business deal.

Local folks usually drop in at Arnaud's for lunch on Fridays. The fun thing is the twist on the old and new cocktail program. It is indeed a walk back in time; because they've been so artful in keeping with the 1920s theme, I feel like you could order a drink the way they did a century ago—and it would be the same!

FRENCH 75

1½ oz. Courvoisier VS Cognac

1 tsp. fresh lemon juice

¼ tsp. simple syrup

2¾ oz. Moët & Chandon Champagne

Lemon twist, to garnish

1. Place the cognac, lemon juice, and simple syrup in a cocktail shaker filled with ice and shake only long enough to chill. Pour into a chilled champagne glass.
2. Top with the Champagne.
3. Garnish with the lemon twist.

CAROUSEL BAR & LOUNGE

214 Royal Street (in the Hotel Monteleone)
New Orleans, LA 70130

If you are looking to relax and wind down, this is not the bar. Instead, you'll find dozens of people who come to network, socialize, and listen to great local jazz music while elbowing their way to the now-famous rotating bar, which is an actual merry-go-round. It's always busy, and it's a long-time popular hot spot, to be sure. If you get a coveted seat at the spinning bar, consider yourself lucky because that area is usually standing room only. Historic and fanciful Royal Street is visible through a glass window wall, which is particularly cool.

The bar is best known for the Vieux Carré (say *view-care-eh*), a cocktail invented in 1938 to honor the many diverse cultures that made up the French Quarter at that time. The drink list appropriately has all of the New Orleans classics, plus some fanciful interpretations. For instance, you can you get the Sazerac or the Sazerac de Forge (which will set you back $90), made with cognac, Nouvelle-Orléans Absinthe Supérieure, and Peychaud's Bitters, as well as two different takes on the Old Fashioned. The options are whimsical yet solid and meld French flair with the romance of the French Quarter.

DRINK LIKE A LOCAL: NEW ORLEANS

Be warned, it's probably not the carousel that's gonna get you dizzy, as it only makes a full turn every fifteen minutes. Blame it on the alcohol. It's more likely the drinks that will have you spinning and having a good old time.

VIEUX CARRÉ

2 teaspoons of D.O.M. Bénédictine

¼ oz. cognac

½ oz. Sazerac Rye Whiskey

¼ oz. sweet vermouth

3 drops Angostura Bitters

2 drops Peychaud's Bitters

Lemon twist, to garnish

1. Put all the ingredients (except the lemon twist) in a mixing glass with ice, and stir until well blended.
2. Pour over ice in a rocks glass.
3. Garnish with the lemon twist.

THE WILL & THE WAY

719 Toulouse Street
New Orleans, LA 70130

The bartenders are the stars behind the bar and, boy, do they put on a show, steadily mixing over-the-top cocktails without ego…even though they'd be within their rights to have big ones. They move with knowledgeable grace, mixing and pouring their list of classic cocktails. They are creative, on point, and so much fun to watch. In fact, some of them kinda look like rock stars, with long locks, cool chains, trendy hairdos, beanie caps, black gear, ponytails, and big-ass smiles.

The menu is a spirited listing of fun drinks. Slipping into a cozy nook is easy, as a row of accent candles leads us there. You can get lost here—are we in New Orleans? The eighteenth-century architecture and outdoor courtyard tell us so. It's an eclectic atmosphere in a converted Creole cottage that dates back to 1794. Everything from the menu to inspirational quotes are written with chalk on the dark walls. Tonight we are rocking out to hipster beats and barroom classics. One guy, as he leaves, simulates playing an air guitar like he was on stage. I look around and smile, knowing the team here has created a lil slice of alternative happiness with their personalities, love of spirits, and passion for the industry.

Little known fact: This is a great place for double dating or late-night sipping, with drinks inspired by in-house infused syrups, including a rotating selection of frozen drinks.

Walking in you could be greeted with everything from "hey, dude" or "hi, homie" to "welcome, friend." Either way, this place is a vibe, and you'd be remiss if you didn't catch it. Like the quote on the chalkboard wall says, "Do cool shit and stay humble, Teach and create contagious joy." Since opening one year after the pandemic hit, this team has done exactly that, and they are going strong.

LAFITTE'S BLACKSMITH SHOP BAR

941 Bourbon Street
New Orleans, LA 70116

It's not unusual to stumble into this corner lot bar. We've been here for Mardi Gras, as well as any given day of the week. Whenever you arrive, you are sure to find a crowd roaring with laughter or dancing outside, drink in hand, of course. It's a great "grab and go" place.

The history here is like no other. Dating back to the early 1700s, it's said to be the oldest building housing a bar in the United States. The Lafitte brothers were black-smiths, spies, and pirates. The blacksmith shop opened as a legitimate storefront that also smuggled goods from the Mississippi River. The cypress wood and brick are original and beautiful in their worn but wonderful appeal. Also still inside is the original blacksmith fireplace, where who knows what was made there, as the stories vary depending on who you ask. Lafitte's is famous for the Purple Voodoo Daiquiri (aka "the Purple Drank"), which is sure to put a spell on you. Its slushy, sweet grape flavor is spiked with bourbon and very powerful. This is not the place to ask for a craft cocktail.

Like several other places in the French Quarter, Lafitte's is said to be haunted, possibly by Jean Lafitte himself, sitting at the fireplace or in the back room by the piano bar. Maybe that's why most everyone is outside—drinking, dancing, and in complete awe of its ghosts, grape drinks, and profound history.

MOLLY'S AT THE MARKET

1107 Decatur Street
New Orleans, LA 70116

"Good morning," says the bartender. No matter that it's 9:02 p.m. Most people have been here since ten this morning. Some of the most hysterical and over-the-top spirited characters in the French Quarter tend bar here. I discovered Molly's during my news anchor days, because traditionally this is a press bar where media hang out and have done so since 1974.

This is a third-generation, family-owned business, open every day until at least 3 a.m. The drink menu is casual with cheap prices, which is unusual for the French Quarter. It's uniquely the place that hosts an equal number of locals and tourists. You might think the loud talking will spark an argument, but it's just the opposite—it's more likely a spirited debate or folks poking fun at each other.

Eventually everyone comes through here, from musicians and politicians to athletes and actors. It's open every day and is known for heavy pours. My Moscow Mules are kicking.

If these old walls could talk, they would tell the stories of the many years' worth of collectibles that hang from them; there are old photos, football helmets, trophies, a large poster of Pope Pius XI, and an occupied urn...who's in there?

This divey Irish pub was one of the first to reopen after Hurricane Katrina in 2005; it operated for many weeks without power yet kept serving drinks. That's where most—if not all—of the hundreds of police badges and ball caps on the bar come from.

We asked the barkeep why locals come here; he says, "We are divey but respectable enough to have a cocktail here. You get it?"

This is a museum of sorts, a keeper of old trinkets and the secrets of tipsy patrons. Drinking here can take you from the crack of dawn to the dusk of night. Leaving, we notice a photo with the last line from a poem by William Butler Yeats: "Cast a cold eye on life, on death. Horseman, pass by." The bartender says it's a reminder to not take life too seriously. In other words, it's a drunk man's version of YOLO. "Cheers, motherf**kers!" he yells out. We look around and most everyone has their glass raised.

NAPOLEON HOUSE

500 Chartres Street
New Orleans, LA 70130

The line outside is wrapped around the building. I think to myself, It's Monday, how could this be? But once you understand the historical relevance of the place, it all makes sense. Visitors come for the traditional classics like the Sazerac, Bourbon Milk Punch, and the bar's signature drink, the Pimm's Cup—and they sell a lot of 'em. Locals come after work or between shifts for the popular New Orleans' muffuletta, a sandwich that is made with cured meats and olive dressing. The classic sandwich pays homage to the Italian immigrants who opened delis in the French Quarter back in the day. Crowds come here for a quick bite and a swig of a special drink.

Napoleon House is a 200-year-old landmark. History buffs will tell you the building was owned by Nicholas Girod, who was mayor of New Orleans from 1812 to 1815, that it served as a hospital during the Civil War, and later had Mafia ties. Legend has it that Girod offered the house to Napoleon as a refuge during his exile. Napoleon never arrived, but the name stuck and is now one of the most famous bars around. As I'm writing this, I'm enamored by the Beethoven music playing, music that was originally created for Napoleon. Our server whispers that it is rumored Tennessee Williams would sit in a candle-lit corner to write and sip, and many other writers came here to find creative inspiration as well.

Fun fact: During Prohibition the bar was a speakeasy, and today the shotgun slot can still be seen aimed at the front door to protect the illegal drinkers. Back then locals would bring their own records to the Imperial Room to drink, dance, and play chess. One of the original chess tables still remains, as does the attraction for folks to sidle up to the bar and make acquaintances.

PIMM'S CUP

1¼ oz. Pimm's No. 1 Liqueur

3 oz. lemonade

Lemon-lime soda

Cucumber slice, to garnish

1. Fill a tall 12-oz. glass with ice. Add the Pimm's and lemonade. Top off with the soda.
2. Garnish with the cucumber slice.

TUJAGUE'S

429 Decatur Street
New Orleans, LA 70130

One of the oldest bars in one of our oldest neighborhoods, Tujague's is popular in so many ways. First of all, it's been in business for 165 years and keeps a tradition of cocktail excellence. It's best known for its signature drink, the Grasshopper, a minty after-dinner sipper named for its light green color. Philip Guichet invented this drink for a 1918 cocktail competition and it became so popular at home in New Orleans that it's been on the menu ever since.

The restaurant has been around before New Orleans got its name. When Prohibition ended, the bar opened. Early rising French Market butchers would come at the crack of dawn to grab a drink and eat, which ultimately led to the creation of "brunch." It was mainly family operated and passed down through generations. In the mid-1960s the bar turned into a clubhouse of sorts for political and well-to-do folks to gather.

The 2020 pandemic forced Tujague's to move from its original location (lease issues), making many of us wonder what would happen to this institution . . . but not to worry, it's now just a few blocks away. It's also bigger, able to hold more than double the number of people. Sadly, they weren't able to take the ornate bar because it was too fragile to survive the trip. But there are a few relics from the original location still hanging on the walls.

It's estimated that the bar serves more than a thousand Grasshoppers on Mardi Gras Day. Let the revelry begin!

GRASSHOPPER

2 oz. heavy cream

¾ oz. dark crème de cacao

¾ oz. light crème de cacao

¾ oz. green crème de menthe

¾ oz. white crème de menthe

½ oz. brandy

1. Shake all of the ingredients, except the brandy, in a cocktail shaker without ice, and strain into a grasshopper glass or champagne flute.
2. Top with the brandy.

PALM & PINE

308 N. Rampart Street
New Orleans, LA 70112

Doors are open and the atmosphere immediately lets you know all are welcome, with rainbow flags, cultural art, and a Black Lives Matter poster up front. We love it here mainly because the cocktail program is over the top with a nice selection of beer and shots. The server told us, "We use funky, original ingredients and infused syrups, although nothing's too sweet. We do a lot of tiki-inspired drinks too." The drinks are wildly creative, and we love drinking here.

One cocktail, the Bomb.com, stands out because 50 percent of the proceeds from its sales are given to the BackStreet Cultural Museum, which houses cultural artifacts and New Orleans' memorabilia—such a good idea! They also have the Kitten Club section, which offers nonalcoholic drinks. It's Southern vibrant to be sure. Adding to the fun is a burlesque show with Bella Blue twice a month.

Palm & Pine is also a great service industry late-night spot—although everyone is welcome.

This bar has had its share of challenges: a two-year street closure due to the collapsed Hard Rock Hotel, a flood, COVID, and Hurricane Ida. Yet, like its namesake the palm, this place and its people are resilient, victorious, peaceful, and symbols of eternal life. We hope they'll be around forever.

BAR TONIQUE

820 N. Rampart Street
New Orleans, LA 70116

This is the ultimate neighborhood cocktail bar. Patrons jam out to funky, hip music, with tapping feet and bobbing heads while perusing the cocktail menu, which includes the classics and a variety of daily specials. It's a humble environment, all encompassed in brick walls, with a centrally located bar and private nooks. The vibe screams diversity. It's minority owned, largely BIPOC and/or LGBTQ+ staffed and true to the mission of equity and inclusion. Visitors and locals love it because the team strives to represent the community it serves.

Bar Tonique sits just on the outskirts of the northern border of the French Quarter, overlooking historic Armstrong Park (named after New Orleans-born jazz legend Louis Armstrong). It's a fitting intersection of location and bar, when you consider the street's history. In the early twentieth century, it was the center of an important African American commercial and entertainment district.

The cocktails here include modern creations as well as authentic pre–Civil War and 1920s recipes. The bar is unpretentious but well respected for its cocktail program, house-made ingredients, happy hour, and stellar staff, who take pride in everything they serve. At 6'4 and 220 pounds, their Old Fashioned had me relaxed and feeling good. It's no wonder locals come here regularly and visitors keep coming back.

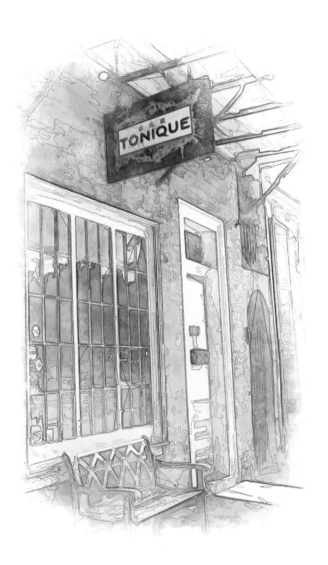

PAT O'BRIEN'S

718 St. Peter
New Orleans, LA 70116

You will make a new friend every time you come. Pat O's—as we call it—isn't exactly a local destination bar (definitely not first on our list), but we find ourselves here more often than not, typically when a friend comes

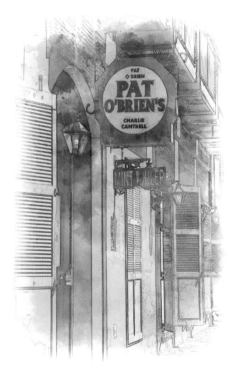

to town, or a visitor exclaims, "We have to go to Pat O'Brien's!" We usually happily shrug and say, "OK, I haven't been there in ages!"

What's not to enjoy? You have to give them their props. There is a fabulous patio, water fountains, and several bars with longtime bartenders and support staff. The Piano Bar is still rocking after all these years. The high energy is contagious, and you'll soon find yourself singing along.

The bar opened in 1933, right after passage of the 21st Amendment, the repeal of Prohibition. Back then, much of the booze came from the Caribbean, where you had to buy large amounts of rum. So they made a drink called the Hurricane, mixed in a little passion fruit and here we are today, sipping on one of New Orleans' most popular drinks. Over the years, many bartenders have put their twist of the world-famous drink, with folks still coming to the original location for it.

PAT O'S HURRICANE

1 oz. gold rum

1 oz. silver rum

1 oz. passion fruit syrup

1 oz. lime juice

Black rum

Maraschino cherry and orange slice, to garnish

1. Shake the gold and silver rum, passion fruit syrup, and lime juice together in a cocktail shaker with ice. Once chilled and mixed, pour all ingredients, including ice, into a Hurricane glass.

2. Use the black rum for float. To make a float, slowly pour black rum onto a piece of ice. It will create the float.

3. Garnish with the cherry and orange slice.

KINGFISH KITCHEN & COCKTAILS

337 Chartres Street
New Orleans, LA 70130

Here we drink like a king. We love coming because Kingfish reminds us of old New Orleans, from the exposed brick to the extra-large picture of Huey P. Long in the entryway, along with one of our state bird (the pelican) and the Huey P. Long Bridge. Who is Huey P. Long, you may wonder? He was Louisiana's fortieth governor, whose nickname was "Kingfish." The bar's name and décor pay homage to his political era. As a champion of the poor, Long's slogan was "Every man a king." His favorite cocktail was the Ramos Gin Fizz.

Closed for more than two years because of the COVID-19 pandemic, it took a lot of work to get the team back in place, but they are better than ever! The bartenders are strapped with suspenders, which adds to the Southern charm. It is a casually romantic place with a long, beautiful U-shaped bar that serves up most of the classics, which are on the Sip List and include the French 75, Pimm's Cup, Sazerac, and Hurricane. The cocktail program is impressive, with good drinks sure to quench your thirst, including recipes from local cocktail legend Chris McMillian. The food menu offers choices like crawfish grilled cheese and red beans and rice with fried chicken, which go well with most any drink we order.

If Huey Long had a reputation of being fiery and spontaneous, we think this bar lives up to that legacy.

BLACK PENNY

700 N. Rampart Street
New Orleans, LA 70116

Just a chill spot: no frills, no jukebox, no TV, no real website. It's a classic, good ol' neighborhood bar with customers who are as comfortable here as it gets. It's like they live here. You'll find a businessman in a dark corner with his computer, friends telling old bar tales, or a sleepy one with his head on the bar. Bartender nudges him and says, "Time to get up, see ya tomorrow." Seems everyone here is familiar and been coming for years.

Black Penny is a late, late-night spot. It's a service industry hangout in the wee morning hours, with most of the business coming between 12:30 a.m. and 4:30 a.m. The team keeps up to fifty different beers on hand, a select variety of high-end alcohol, and the usual stuff. Ask them to make you a cocktail and they will, but they are also likely to suggest a beer!

Brick archways, faded plaster walls, coveted Mardi Gras Zulu coconuts, a menorah, and a rainbow painting all signal everyone is welcome...one love. Among many, there is but one black penny...and, funny, this one is the shiniest.

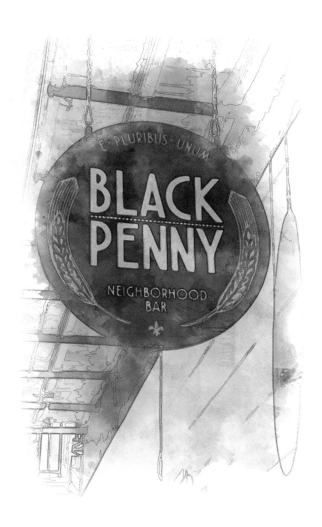

BEACHBUM BERRY'S LATITUDE 29

321 N. Peters Street
New Orleans, LA 70130

It's not every day you walk in and the man with the white goatee, stylish glasses, and raffia beach hat is sitting in the corner entertaining guests. We're like, "No wayyy...tiki's leading man is here." We could tell you about Jeff Berry's emergence into the craft tiki world, his seven tiki books, and tiki-inspired themed bar. But since we've spotted him, we'll let him tell his story.

"Why do you think locals drink here? A big thing is we teach our staff 'aloha' bartending: it's welcoming, full of Southern hospitality. We make 'em feel good when they walk in the door—everything from smiling and making eye contact to simply acknowledging them. 'Aloha' is 50 percent of what keeps them coming back. Twenty-five percent is our unique drink list, and 25 percent is our atmosphere. We took a long time with major attention to detail to give the experience of a mini vacation feel. We created an island getaway for a town that doesn't have a beach.

"My wife and I came to New Orleans in 2005 for the Tales of the Cocktail Convention. When we got off the shuttle bus in front of the Hotel Monteleone, there were musicians, a homogenized culture, and people were

just cool. We were like, 'Where's this place been all of our lives?' We fell in love overnight and said, 'OK, we are moving here.' Then Hurricane Katrina hit and we diverted to North Carolina. But for us, it was always New Orleans. It just took us seven years to get here. Finally, after finding the right location, we opened the first craft cocktail tiki bar here.

What do you want your guests to leave feeling, we ask?

"For one, it's been a hard road since the pandemic. We closed several times. We adjusted to retain staff. Imbibers should know we work really hard to keep up with the changing trends, from new ingredients to cool stuff to garnish with. We only change the menu once a year. I might come in with a great idea, but my team takes it to the next level, adding science and stuff. I rely on them, and I read a lot of cocktail books. We want our drinks to have a spine, with ingredients that enhance, not compete."

Jeff "Beachbum" Berry is so passionate that he researches, creates, and basically lives tropical. He's a trailblazer for tiki culture, and we are in awe of his conviviality. Through a lot of laughter and aloha vibes, we made a new friend...or at least that's how it feels. He's a great host to toast.

DEEP SIX
Serves 2

4 oz. Coruba or Myers's Original Dark Jamaican Rum

1 oz. Hamilton 151 Demerara Overproof Rum

2 oz. fresh lime juice

2 oz. pineapple juice

2½ oz. falernum

1¼ oz. allspice dram

Fresh mint sprig, to garnish

1. Shake all the ingredients, except the mint, together in a cocktail shaker filled with ice cubes. Pour everything, including ice, into a large snifter. Add more ice to fill.

2. Garnish with the mint and serve with two straws.

SYLVAIN

625 Chartres Street
New Orleans, LA 70130

If you want to experience a 1700s carriage house, French neighborhood culture, and modern cocktails, this is it! Is it a bar with a bistro, or a bistro with a great bar? We cannot decide. Even though you'll get a great bite here, the bar menu offers unique twists on many cocktail classics. Be warned: it is small, but intimate and relaxed.

We love the dark décor and mini chandeliers, which add a classy touch. There is a quaint courtyard out back that makes you forget you're in a busy neighborhood.

While the atmosphere is laid-back, the cocktail program is quite the opposite. Bartenders here make their own juices, flavor mixtures, and sodas. They offer several specialty cocktails, none over-the-top garish, just very well made—perhaps even meticulously so.

Fun fact: Sylvain is the former home of New Orleans brothel owner Aunt Rose. Every day before shift, bartenders put a drink on the bar to honor her memory and business savvy. Also, Sylvain is the name of the first opera to be performed in New Orleans. It was raucous and funny…much like what usually happens in this French Quarter hideaway.

MURIEL'S JACKSON SQUARE

801 Chartres Street
New Orleans, LA 70116

We love to bring our out-of-town friends here for fun ghost stories and great drinks in the upstairs Séance Lounge. I've recently started ordering the zero-proof cocktails off their menu and enjoy them just as much. Locals know this location is the heartbeat of the French Quarter, just off the corner of the popular Jackson Square. It's the perfect location to stop in for happy hour or a light libation. The bar is tucked into a hallway courtyard alcove.

The mansion it is located in is older than the city, more than 300 years old. Back in the day, there were grand parties here, lavish affairs that saw the likes of everyone from politicians to pirates. One owner, Pierre Antoine Lepardi Jourdan, bought the property in 1789. Unfortunately, he was a degenerate drunk and gambler, and one night he put the mansion up in a poker game and lost! When it came time to turn over the deed, he hung himself upstairs in the Séance Room. The bartender says his spirit still lives here. Recently she saw a mysterious image of a 1900s-style woman in a customer's photo. Crazy, right? Then she tells us about one night when a liquor bottle flew off the second-story bar ledge, landing right-side up. Even crazier, right? The hostess

told us the glass toothpick holder floated down to the floor, never breaking. She was shocked, but picked it up and kept on working. Because of such goings-on, the staff puts out a glass of wine every night to thank the spirit for allowing folks to come into his home to eat and drink.

The twisted irony is, in a house that Pierre lost, he actually never left. We'll raise a glass to that!

FLEUR DE LIS

1 oz. champagne

1½ oz. raspberry vodka

¾ oz. Chambord

1 oz. orange juice

1 oz. pineapple juice

Orange wedge, to garnish

1. Pour the champagne in a martini glass.
2. Put the raspberry vodka, Chambord, orange juice, and pineapple juice in a cocktail shaker, and shake with ice. Strain over the champagne.
3. Garnish with the orange wedge.

THE CHART ROOM

300 Chartres Street
New Orleans, LA 70130

The king of dive bars pays homage to marine life. You feel like you're in a small boat. There are numerous artifacts from boats and mariners like outdated maps, anchors, and tattered sailor hats. Navigation charts line the walls, hence the name. The bartender told us that during the 1960s, sailors from all over the world would come here to drink and would leave behind some of their home currency; those bills still hang above the bar to this day, tattered and torn.

The bar is tiny, dark, and dingy yet full of character. The backbar is made of barge board from a waterlogged boat out of the Mississippi River. Once undesirable, it's now popular to use barge wood in the renovation of Creole cottages throughout New Orleans. The edge of the bar is worn, likely from the many elbows that have rubbed against it over the years.

What's to drink? The basics at a cheap price. No fancy glasses, no frills, just drinks and a lot of stories. Ask for Chris, who comically tells stories of past and present. You'll never forget your conversation with him. He claims to have the coolest memorabilia of any bar in the world. He'll point to a framed picture that shows the bar's bumper sticker on the US space shuttle *Atlantis*, a deal that was conjured up with astronauts who came to drink one night. Lo and behold, they held up their end of the bargain, and The Chart Room sticker appeared on the shuttle's window.

Fun fact: Ray Newman owned the bar for forty years before passing in 2014. The story goes that he was a big gambler and won his ownership of it in a gin rummy game. True? We don't really know, but it makes for interesting lore.

Hospitality folks come here after work, and there's a jukebox with New Orleans' music and old-school hits. This is a cash-only neighborhood bar. There are no rules here, except "No assholes allowed."

DAVENPORT LOUNGE

921 Canal Street (in the Ritz-Carlton)
New Orleans, LA 70112

Located inside the Ritz-Carlton, you might not think it's exactly a locals' kinda place, but *au contraire*. On the third floor, past the lobby, is an upscale open-bar lounge with bartenders we have known for decades. Not only do the bartenders keep us coming, the main attraction is the band, led by Jeremy Davenport. They have been gracing the stage for years, and they keep us on the dance floor. The bar was named after Jeremy, a tremendous trumpet player. The band is locally famous, and imbibers support them while drinking high-end drinks in elegant, lively surroundings. Try the Davenportini, a crowd favorite.

Yes, it's fancy in a Ritz Carlton kind of way. Under amber, lit chandeliers, you can sit back in cozy couch sections, leather chairs, or at the long bar. The music will keep you coming back, and the drinks will satisfy your thirst.

CUBAN CREATIONS CIGAR BAR

533 Toulouse Street
New Orleans, LA 70130

If you're looking for a stogie and a sip, you've landed in the right place. This old bathhouse has been transformed into a luxe cigar lounge, a great place to "tap dat ash," as they say. Even better, it has been grandfathered in to allow indoor smoking, with top-notch ventilation. Open every day, it's the only cigar bar in the French Quarter. It has top-of-the-line cigar lockers and a custom walk-in humidor made from Spanish cedar.

There are two domino tables, and the back room has a Las Vegas feel, with large columns, sky-blue-painted ceilings, big-screen TVs, and nice furniture. We enjoy watching sports here, falling comfortably into the large black leather chairs.

You'll find locals, politicians, athletes, and a handful of tourists here. NBA legend Karl Malone comes in from time to time and his La Aurora smokes are sold here.

There is no cocktail menu; most drinks are made to order.

CUBAN MOJITO

1½ oz. Don Q Cristal Rum

3 raw sugar cubes

1 healthy sprig fresh mint

1 oz. fresh lime juice

Soda water

Sprite soda

Fresh mint leaf, to garnish

Lime wedge, to garnish

1. Muddle the rum, sugar cubes, mint sprig, and lime juice together in a mixing glass. Pour over crushed ice into a copper mug.
2. Top with the soda water and Sprite.
3. Garnish with the mint and lime.

More French Quarter Favorites

EFFERVESCENCE BUBBLES AND BITES
1036 N. Rampart Street

If you like bubbles like we do, this champagne bar is exactly what you need. Not only is it "crazy sexy cool" as we like to say, its design is modern and sleek. Great outdoor patio. Try the champagne flights.

GOOD FRIENDS BAR
740 Dauphine Street

Really cheap well drinks, and the corner entryway is always filled with festive folks at this French Quarter gay bar. The famous Separator drink is coffee, liquor, and ice cream topped with whipped cream. Upstairs is the Queens Head Pub, which is more Victorian in design with fancy chandeliers and candelabras. The motto: "Good drinks. Good times. Good friends meet here." This is a true local hang out.

PEYCHAUD'S
727 Toulouse Street

If the courtyard in front of the bar isn't enough, the location will take your breath away. Once the home of Antoine Amedee Peychaud, who created the famous bitters, we come here for a back-in-the-day feel and drinks that use authentic ingredients.

HARRY'S CORNER BAR
900 Chartres Street

A true low-key vibe, which is a little odd for a French Quarter neighborhood dive bar. Windows are always open, and this is a great place to drink and people watch. Beer, wine and drinks are cheap. Bring cash only.

CANE & TABLE
1113 Decatur Street

A great place to stop and imbibe while walking the Quarter. It has a long wrap-around bar and outdoor tables. Most cocktail ingredients like syrups and bitters are made in house and may cost a bit more, but the quality is worth it.

OZ
800 Bourbon Street

Get ready to dance the night away in this popular gay bar. It has two stories, a balcony, and two bars. Drinks are reasonably priced and pretty simple. Don't ask for a craft cocktail here, but there are decent wine options.

COSIMO'S
1201 Burgundy Street

Tucked away in a great neighborhood on the edge of the French Quarter, this bar is unassuming and bigger than it looks. It has a pool table and cheap drinks.

MRB BAR & KITCHEN
515 St. Phillip Street

Catch local bands, oysters, and more than 100 beers, many of them local. They dare you to try the frozen "Green Drank." The bar's name stands for "Mississippi River Bottom." We never pass the yellow sign without stopping in for a drink, and it's a frequent stop for us during crawfish season. We load up on oysters and beer (or Bloody Marys) and sit in the courtyard. It's a former speakeasy, and some say it's one of the most haunted bars in the city.

FRENCH QUARTER

FAUBOURG MARIGNY

The Marigny, adjacent to the French Quarter, is a vibrant historic neighborhood full of funky live music venues, art, cafes, beautiful architecture, and businesses. There are plenty of wine bistros, jazz clubs, and late-night bars. We love the sidewalk musicians, brass bands, and the hipster vibe, especially along Frenchman Street, which is often called "the locals' Bourbon Street."

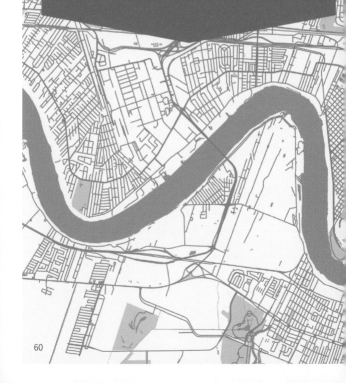

Mid-City

Gentilly

Treme

Marigny

Bywater

French
Quarter

Central
Business
District

Garden
District

Uptown

Irish
Channel

61

PEPP'S PUB

706 Franklin Avenue
New Orleans, LA 70117

The bar is named after the owners' Labrador–German Shepherd mix dog named Pepper. They bought the bar the Mardi Gras before the COVID shutdown in 2020 and made it through by the hair of their chinny chin chins. They decided to take the forced time off to renovate, which is when they discovered hidden barge board walls and a huge front window covered with wood. Now it's a bit more open, with an outdoor patio.

These folks take "dog friendly" to the next level, so much so that dogs bring their owners here. There are dog murals, Polaroids of dogs in gold frames, framed doggy bones, and free doggie treats next to a cooler labeled "people water."

We join the outrageously large crowds here for the popular Intergalactic Krewe of Chewbacchus, St. Anne, and the satirical Krewe du Vieux Carnival parades. We sip on the "Crushes," made with fresh-squeezed grapefruit and orange juice.

They host monthly dog rescues and art markets. There is a real community connection here. A guy plopped down next to us and said, "You look like my dad thirty years ago." One thing led to another, tequila shots were thrown back, and the debate ensued—the correct pronunciation of New Orleans streets. Is it Calliope...or Ca-lye-a-pee? Burgundy or Burr-gun-dee?

We love the family atmosphere. As we settle in, patrons yell, "Good night, Richard!" (the bartender on duty) and he responds, "See ya later, baby." Indeed, you will see us soon.

THE ELYSIAN BAR

2317 Burgundy Street
(inside the Hotel Peter and Paul)
New Orleans, LA 70117

It's the rebirth of a grand nineteenth-century historic Catholic church, rectory, and schoolhouse. Inside the Hotel Peter and Paul sits The Elysian Bar, which is where the rectory once was. We adore the four sitting rooms that priests once called home. The $20 million renovation was clearly more than a facelift, it was an exclamation point on the overall campus resurrection. Every detail has been considered, every seat is dainty...small, like you might imagine the people back then were. The parlors have working fireplaces, and antiques are all around. Some of the nooks remind me of slightly larger confessionals. The atrium is full of windows for sunlight or moonlight to spill through and lots of hanging plants, all of which makes it easy for me to sit back, sip on my Spritz, and consider my blessings.

At the actual bar you sit under a lifelike bald cypress, the official tree of Louisiana. It is the focal point of the bar and quite the piece of art. The tree design is the work of artists at Mardi Gras World (the amazing creators of the city's over-the-top Mardi Gras parade floats and costumes). Don't miss the red leather barstools and all-star alcohol lineup. It's cozy and quaint. Perhaps the most interesting thing of all is that the people around the bar are not necessarily hotel guests; they're likely to be locals.

This space has a kind of magic. If these walls could talk, I imagine they'd keep us up all night with tales of splendor and maybe a little sin.

LINNEA'S GARDEN

6 dashes orange bitters

½ oz. passion fruit liqueur

½ oz. Cappelletti Aperitivo

1½ oz. Berto Vermouth Bianco

2 oz. sparkling rosé

Edible flower, to garnish (optional)

1. Build in a wine glass starting with the bitters, then add ice, then the passion fruit liqueur, Cappelletti Aperitivo, and Berto Blanco and top with the sparkling rosé.

2. Garnish with the flower, if you like.

NEW ORLEANS ART BAR

2128 St. Claude Avenue
New Orleans, LA 70116

Fairly new to the cocktail scene, this is a bookstore/ speakeasy in the Marigny neighborhood, full of flair, sexiness, and consciousness. Locals come to hear authors and poets read and talk about their work while sipping on the good stuff, everything from high-end wine, craft cocktails, and brews to zero-proof drinks. We love the vodka-based Elysian Beauty, with its hint of hibiscus, and the tequila-fueled The Devil Finds Work, with lime and bitters. Sooo good.

This place is like walking into a literary dream, with everything from self-help, autobiographies, and children's books to Black girl magic and novels. What's better than burying your nose in the pages of classics and new releases, while having healthy debates and partying all the while? The courtyard is shared with Baldwin & Co. Bookstore (same owners).

The wall art is all local. They rotate artists every four months and, if the price is right, it's yours to take home. There is a weekly art market, tarot card readings, Afrobeats, DJs, and live music. So sip and shop, socialize, and consider joining the book club at this library bar. Drink in hand, of course.

BUD RIP'S

900 Piety Street
New Orleans, LA 70117

Where the big hearts meet…that's what is written in fancy calligraphy on the outside of the building on the corner of Burgundy and Piety Streets in the Upper Ninth Ward/Bywater neighborhood.

The rock 'n' roll music ricochets off the high tin-tiled ceiling, and the disco light swirls around as if to move to the music. The pink-and-orange globe lights keep our attention. There are plenty of beers and shots to go around. There are about a dozen beers on tap and one big TV above the long ornate bar.

Bud Rip's is the third oldest bar in New Orleans. Edward "Bud Rip" Ripoll Jr. owned the bar for thirty-five years. It sits across the street from the original Schwegmann's, an iconic grocery store that no longer exists. The bar first opened in 1860 as a spot for wharf men and long-shoremen.

The bartender tells us that back in the day, women were not allowed to drink inside, so they had to order from an outside window. There were hints, she says, of gender and cultural racism. But the new ownership squashed all that. Now it's open to everyone and as inclusive as it gets.

There's nothing but puppy love here. Dogs sit on the leather benches and drink doggie drinks at the bar. As for us humans, it's a great place to end the night, as it's open late, 3 a.m. on weekends.

So, go in and slip into one of the long leather benches and jukebox jam. Maybe shoot some pool. It's a natural stop for regulars who likely walk there or ride their bikes. The neighborhood supports it, even after the tourist season is over.

THE SPOTTED CAT MUSIC CLUB

623 Frenchmen Street
New Orleans, LA 70117

A great little place on Frenchman Street. Are you ready to get down to jazz, blues, and gypsy swing? There is a never-ending stream of sultry sounds pouring out of the doorway and open window. Musicians here are always playing their hearts out. You can cram inside and jam with the others, or grab a seat outside in the small patio area. This funky bar has been around since 2000. Be warned: it's cash only, no reservations, and you're sure to be served in a plastic cup. There is a one-drink minimum, and the drinks are relatively cheap.

If you want to sit down, you'd better come early, as it fills up quickly, especially on weekends. You can hear a variety of bands, solo artists, and some big voices. You may be lucky enough to see a swing dancer or two.

This bar is authentic, shabby, and looks a bit fatigued, but don't be fooled. The energy is high, the crowds are plentiful, and, although it is small, it provides a robust experience. Be sure to push your way to the front to get closer to the bands. Sip slowly because the pours are plentiful. It's known by us locals simply as "The Cat."

SNUG HARBOR JAZZ BISTRO

626 Frenchmen Street
New Orleans, LA 70116

Looking for a jazzy night? This is the best of both worlds. New Orleans is known as the birthplace of jazz and cocktails, and when you mix the two under one roof, you have hit nirvana. We are always drawn to the brick-encased bar with abstract paintings of famous artists who've performed here. There is a music concert room where some of the most talented musicians, both local and global, come to wow the crowds. If you are not in the intimate jazz listening room, you can watch the live performances on the TVs around the bar. Imagine sipping on wine, beer, or cocktails while swaying to the rhythms of jazz. Try Papa's Rum Runner; Snug Harbor is the only place in town to date that carries Papa's Pilar Rum.

Many will tell you memories of grabbing a brew and a burger to coat their tummies before a long night out perusing the Frenchman Street music district. We love Snug Harbor because we see so many progressive jazz legends, from the locally iconic Charmaine Neville (and family) to jazz drummer Jason Marsalis and countless brass bands.

The atmosphere here removes our inhibitions, and it moves us in a way only the music of New Orleans can. We allow our feet to tap to the beat, listen to the trombone moan, and sip, sip, sip the night away.

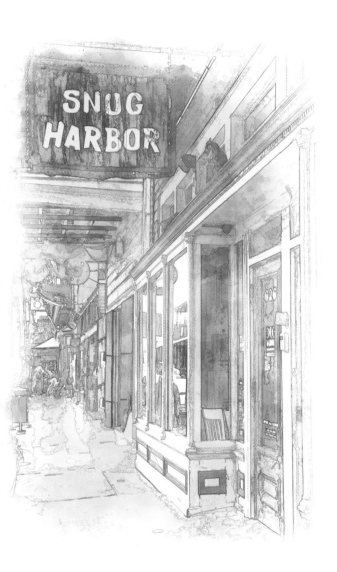

More Faubourg Marigny Favorites

THE R BAR
1431 Royal Street

The energy here is so lackadaisical, it's contagious. There are always groups outside having
inexpensive drinks—$2 Highlife, to be exact.
Inside, there's a barber's chair if you need a
quick $10 snip and a shot, a fake fox wearing a
leather jacket, a pool table, and a jukebox. Often
there are food pop-ups. A lot of millennials
roam through to mingle with the old heads.

HI-HO LOUNGE
2239 St. Claude Avenue

We always stumble here and think, Oh yeah,
haven't been here in a while. Always fun, great
live music, and inexpensive drinks. Definitely a
neighborhood joint with an underground vibe.
Sometimes there's jazz, other nights it's zydeco.
Either way try not to miss the $1 red beans and
rice night.

EMPORIUM ARCADE BAR
2231 St. Claude Avenue

Who doesn't love a good arcade bar? A great open-air space with dozens of vintage video games, hoops, pool, pinball, and more with a decent drink list.

THE MAISON
508 Frenchmen Street

When there is a good band playing, we pack the place and happily drink out of plastic cups while dancing the night away. It has three floors, so there are plenty of places to sit and spread out and enjoy the entertainment. Good wine and beer selection.

DBA
618 Frenchmen Street

The bar is on one side, live music is on the other. The chalkboard menu hangs high above the bar and shows dozens of craft beers. Great place to see a live show and be social while sipping.

DRAGON'S DEN
435 Esplanade Avenue

It's dark inside and full of hipsters looking for good music and cheap drinks. There is a full calendar of live music and a balcony overlooking the historic Esplanade Avenue.

BYWATER

This neighborhood sits right between the Marigny and the Ninth Ward and is snuggled near the Mississippi River. The area is known for shotgun style houses, fun bars, great eats, and laid-back nightlife. Its nickname is "Sliver by the River" because it doesn't flood here, not even during hurricanes.

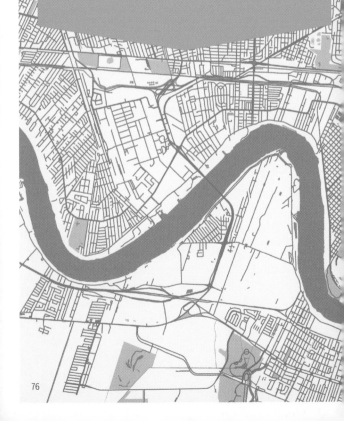

THE COUNTRY CLUB

634 Louisa Street
New Orleans, LA 70117

Hidden away in the Bywater neighborhood is a resort/country club-style bar with everything you can imagine. Local artist Cindy Mathis exploded her creative talent on almost every wall. The Bird Room mural has whimsically-drawn birds in flight, one with a French fry in its mouth, and there is a little bird's nest in the corner. We love flying into the Butterfly Room, as it has Louis St. Lewis's art prominently displayed. If you look closely, some of the butterflies have the faces of the bar's managers on them. The double parlor has gigantic flower murals. All of it is enough to put us in the middle of an abstract wonderland where our minds are at ease.

The bar itself is a square walk-around, inclusive of a wine cellar and floating digital billboard menu. High-back comfy chairs keep us sitting for a while. There is an adequate list of bartender selections, as well as seasonal cocktails that get changed out twice a year. There is a weekly Drag Brunch—reserve ASAP because it sells out fast.

The really special part is the large outdoor saltwater pool (seasonally heated or cooled) with a poolside cabana bar. You can imagine yourself relaxing here for hours, sipping the day or night away. The pool area sports more than 100 lounge chairs as well as fire pits, a twenty-person hot tub, an outdoor grill kitchen, sauna, and a secret garden with TVs for sports lovers and a tranquil fishpond.

It's a fun escape at this 1884 Italianate mansion that was originally a home before becoming a taxi cab hub, a boarding house, and then finally the ultimate neighborhood cocktail bar where we love to sip and socialize.

LA OLD FASHIONED

1 oz. whiskey (they use Old Soul Bourbon from Cathead Distillery)

1 oz. spiced rum (they use False River Spiced Rum)

4 dashes chicory bitters (aromatic bitters could also be substituted)

1 large cube of frozen coconut water

Orange peel, to garnish

1. Combine all the ingredients, except the orange peel, in a rocks glass and stir together.

2. Garnish with the orange peel.

BACCHANAL FINE WINE & SPIRITS

600 Poland Avenue
New Orleans, LA 70117

By definition a bacchanal is an occasion of wild and drunken revelry. But here we call it a normal day full of music, food, and vino! The front door opens into a small, quaint corner shop with wines from all over the world. Go through the double doors that lead outside, and you'll find yourself in a large open-air backyard of sorts, with string lights, black wrought-iron tables and chairs, picnic tables, and a small stage for local bands.

I've made this journey many times since Bacchanal opened in 2002, and with every visit I find a new favorite jazz band, a new wine, and even make a new pal. I've been here for going-away parties, birthday gatherings, anniversary toasts, and more. I can remember its beginnings: a shabby wine shop, pop-up chefs (long before pop-ups were popular), and entertainment that included everything from up-and-coming poets to dancers and solo artists. I can even remember, some years after Hurricane Katrina, when they were shut down for operating without proper permits. The neighborhood rallied, and eventually they won the battle to reopen. What an evolution.

Bacchanal is a favorite mainly because what it is isn't entirely clear. A wine bar? A restaurant? Outdoor concert venue? Creole patio? Whatever it is, it came together serendipitously and we like it, no matter what. The wine list is vast (think about joining their monthly wine subscription), there is a "standing room only" balcony view, and a small indoor room with ivy plants hanging on every wall. I love ivy because it symbolizes resilience—it never dies. This Ninth Ward alfresco bar has all of the natural elements to make for an enchanted evening in the moonlight.

The menu changes all the time. The food is good too, and includes a build-your-own cheese plate. Be warned, you cannot make a reservation—ever—so best to come early! You are likely to find groups of friends standing around, jamming to the jazz. We suggest you catch a ride since neighborhood parking spaces are hard to come by, and you just might get towed if you block the wrong driveway by accident.

MARKEY'S BAR

640 Louisa Street
New Orleans, LA 70117

I walk in the door and already the bartender puts my usual drink in front of me and asks, "How's your day been, sweetie?" Markey's has been in the family for what seems like forever, and it's been in the neighborhood for 114 years. It opened as the Standard Brewing Company, then later became Frisch's Cafe, and in 1947 one of the family members turned it into a bar. The owners live a stone's throw away; they also own the nearby park and have created a place where almost everyone knows everyone. We come to watch sports on the more-than-dozen TVs they have, and we love the low drink prices.

You're likely to see a neighbor or a local musician sipping on a beer before or after a gig. It's not unusual to see someone stopping in for a nightcap while walking their dog. No need to dress up, it's come as you are. You'll see fun socks, flip-flops, camouflage cargo shorts, blue wigs, and anything else anyone feels like wearing. Many nights are spent playing darts or shuffleboard. The neighborhood is quiet, and there is a sign that reminds us to respect that peace—or else.

Markey's is open every day, even Christmas. The history gives this place a sprinkle of charm, but it's the lovable motley crew of people who come here that gives it the nod of approval and the title of one of NOLA's favorite Irish dive bars.

More Bywater Favorites

ALLWAYS LOUNGE & CABARET
2240 St. Claude Avenue

Locals love it here for fun and on any given night will enjoy music, comedy, theater, or a burlesque show (often quite risqué ones).

VAUGHAN'S LOUNGE
4229 Dauphine Street

It's the place you have to remind yourself to go to and when you get there, you remember exactly why. This shabby dive hasn't changed a bit and probably never will. You'll dance, enjoy the local crowd, and order cheap drinks. I'm not sure how to describe the décor as you'll see everything from Carnival tinsel to Christmas lights. Just take it all in and enjoy.

THE FRANKLIN
2600 Dauphine Street

Once you step inside, you get a whiff of what this place is all about. The outside looks like the average Creole cottage but the energy inside will keep you coming back, thanks to the spirited staff and neighborhood characters. Great wine list and heavy pours.

SATURN BAR
3067 St. Claude Avenue

It has a bit of a hipster-meets-rocker type vibe—it's weird and clever at the same time. Be sure to check out the murals and local artwork. Heavy on punk rock.

PARLEAUX BEER LAB
634 Lesseps Street

A craft beer drinker's dream. A great neighborhood taproom with colorful fun indoor and garden-style outdoor seating.

BYWATER BREW PUB
3000 Royal Street

Twelve taps brewed locally, flights, growlers, cocktails, and wine. Super fun environment with trivia on Mondays.

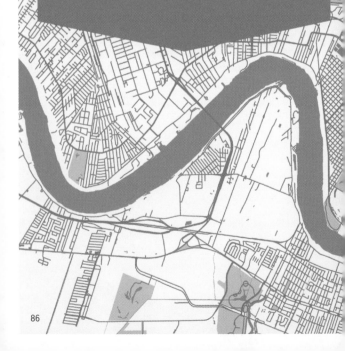

TREME

Pronounced *treh-may* this is one of America's oldest African American neighborhoods. It's north of the French Quarter and is best known for being home to free people of color in the early eighteenth and nineteenth centuries. So much of what makes New Orleans great comes from the Treme—everything from the music, art, Creole food, and that *je ne sais quoi* that reminds you why NOLA is so darn special. From jazz clubs to bars, cultural centers, and soul food, Treme is the source of New Orleans' Black culture.

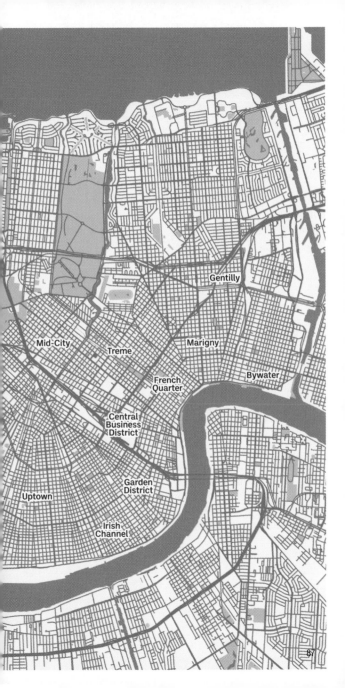

Mid-City

Treme

Gentilly

Marigny

Bywater

French
Quarter

Central
Business
District

Uptown

Garden
District

Irish
Channel

KERMIT'S TREME MOTHER IN LAW LOUNGE

1500 N. Claiborne Avenue
New Orleans, LA 70116

This local spot is owned by native son and famous trumpeter Kermit Ruffins. We have followed his career over the years, and now we go to his bar for cheap drinks, live music, and sometimes free food. You could be lucky enough to catch crawfish served at night, or Kermit himself may be cooking turkey necks and red beans or barbecuing out of the back of his truck.

We have been here several times to watch second line parades. It's also a place where Mardi Gras Indians get together often. You never know what you'll encounter. One night we bumped into a stripper pole in the middle of the room with dollar bills on the floor. Another night, we partied with the cast of the hit show *Greenleaf*. Kermit likes to have fun...and that, he does. Local music fans come to imbibe, and if you're curious enough to visit, you could catch the man himself sitting in a corner watching all the action.

They do have TVs for watching sports or local news. During the COVID pandemic, the city shut Kermit down for continuing to operate. He says he just wanted to give people something to lift their spirits. The lounge has what Kermit calls "the feeling of home and a picnic state of mind." Music, food, beer, friends, repeat. As Kermit says, what's better than being a cultural icon who plays and cooks? "All aboard!!!" he yells, and the crowds know exactly what to do. It signals the beginning of his show and time for you to grab a drink and hit the dance floor.

WHISKEY & STICKS

2513 Bayou Road
New Orleans, LA 70119

The mission here is to serve the best whiskeys and cigars NOLA has ever seen. Perfectly positioned on the oldest road in the city, Whiskey & Sticks is just one of a host of Black-owned businesses along this cultural corridor. Some say New Orleans would not exist were it not for Bayou Road. The business part of the brick-lined road keeps with the city's long history of minority-owned businesses.

Today Whiskey & Sticks is owned by media personalities Ken Jones and Kelder Summers. It is a popular hot spot for fun folks who enjoy a sensational sip and a fine cigar. Located in Treme, the oldest African American neighborhood in the country, this gathering place appeals to sophisticated sippers and makes you feel like you could be in your favorite cousin's den. One visit and you're sure to see a familiar face, because this is where people come to have conversations, talk about the latest and greatest happenings, or take part in weekly trivia night. The art displayed on the walls is culturally relevant and includes pics of Mardi Gras Indians, famous local faces, fun times, and musical icons.

There are three humidors, specialty bourbons, a handful of craft drinks, and—since we cannot smoke inside—a large backyard patio, complete with a stage, TVs, and all the comforts of home, including an outdoor air conditioner for our sweltering summer days.

Good whiskey is meant to be cared for, savored, and sipped with friends. A visit here is simply a taste of the good life.

KEYS TO THE CITY

4 strawberries, sliced, plus more to garnish

2 oz. bourbon or whiskey of your choice

3 oz. lemonade

Fresh mint sprig, to garnish

1. Muddle the strawberries in a mixing glass. Add ice, followed by the bourbon. Pour this mixure, including ice, into a rocks glass. Top with the lemonade.

2. Garnish with strawberry slices. Rub the mint between your fingers, and lay on the surface of the drink.

More Treme Favorites

DON VILLAVASO ON THE BAYOU
3111 Grand Route St. John

Nothing but sticks and swigs. Getting lit never looked so good at the cigar bar that sits along the historic Esplanade Avenue. Grab a stogie from the walk-in humidor, and sip a cognac or whiskey on the outdoor patio.

BULLET'S SPORTS BAR
2441 A P Tureaud Avenue

If you know, you know. Bullet's has been around for what seems like forever on this street named for civil rights attorney A. P. Turead, who was known for battling Jim Crow laws. A place where we see our neighbors, their kids, maybe their *parano*—New Orleans lingo for "godfather." A great place to grab a bucket of beer and one of two things happen: we watch sports or catch some of the best jazz bands in town.

DRINK LIKE A LOCAL: NEW ORLEANS

CANDLELIGHT LOUNGE
925 N Robertson

This longstanding neighborhood dive bar is good for a late-night visit on your way home for live music, brass bands, and basic drinks.

THE LITTLE PEOPLES PLACE
1226 Barracks Street

Only one room, with low ceilings, yet it's out of this world with fun characters and lots of culture. If you don't know the location, you may just pass it by.

POOR BOYS BAR
1328 St. Bernard Avenue

Simple, dark, and loud with live DJs and dancing. Fun for cheap drinks and late-night adventures, as it closes anywhere between 4 and 6 a.m.

DOWNTOWN AND CENTRAL BUSINESS DISTRICT

A bustling neighborhood centrally located and commonly referred to as "the area along the Mississippi River." There are plenty of upscale, sports, and dive bars, lounges, restaurants, fun happy hours, and trendy restaurants.

Mid-City

Gentilly

Treme

Marigny

French
Quarter

Bywater

Central
Business
District

Uptown

Garden
District

Irish
Channel

CHANDELIER BAR

2 Canal Street (inside the Four Seasons Hotel)
New Orleans, LA 70130

If you find yourself at the foot of Canal Street, along the banks of the mighty Mississippi River, it would only be natural to saunter into the elegant and refined Chandelier Bar in the Four Seasons Hotel. The name doesn't disappoint, as it has the most over-the-top fabulous chandelier we've ever seen. As you walk into the hotel, you will see the bar in the center of the lobby. At first glance her glamour might feel a little intimidating. Should I approach? Will I be let in? She is beautiful, to be sure, with higher-than-average bar prices and people all dressed up. As spellbound as we are, we are careful not to be seduced by the magic of the sparking 15,000-crystal chandelier. You can come as you are, by which I mean, Four Seasons "as you are."

The bar is tastefully done, inside and out—be sure to check out the courtyard. We have come here for all sorts of events, meetups, and meetings. If someone invites you here, it's likely for a good reason and probably something special. My girlfriends and I had our holiday gift exchange and cocktail party at the center table some years ago. The social media pics are still some of my favorites.

You might not see the same locals here all the time; the rotation is heavy. We always see groups of friends creating memories.

BARCADIA

601 Tchoupitoulas Street
New Orleans, LA 70130

The fun starts before you walk in the door. Hyped-up music, fun games like cornhole and Jenga, old and modern arcade games, and punching bags, plus energized bartenders all in your face…and we haven't even made it to the bar yet.

The garage door is thrown up to expose a window bar, perfect for people watching. The décor is over the top; don't be surprised if the Mardi Gras decorations are up year-round. This adult arcade has DJs, live music, and trendy tunes piping through. It appears the owners have channeled the best of their childhoods all under one roof. The patio area is usually filled up on the weekends, and there is a live venue in the back called Ohm Lounge.

There isn't a creative cocktail list—it's just the usual stuff: vodka, whiskey, gin, Red Bull, etc. This is a high-volume spot with a young vibe where you can dance, socialize, and hang with large groups of friends.

BAR MARILOU

544 Carondelet Street
New Orleans, LA 70130

The sexy, dimly-lit salon bar is in the old library of what was the city hall annex and is now a quaint hideaway with bookshelves everywhere, serving sophisticated cocktails with a French flair you simply can't ignore. Even on the busiest nights it has a relaxed feeling. On our designated date nights, this is at the top of our list mainly because we can slip into a cozy cove surrounded by candles and be inspired by the romantic setting.

You enter the bar by going down a garden-like walkway adorned with iron gates. Its décor is deep scarlet red, from top to bottom, with a leopard-patterned carpet. There is a swinging door cleverly disguised as a book-shelf that opens into a sumptuous private salon with seating for twelve; everyone is curious to peek inside, but it's for hotel guests only.

The cocktail menu oozes European influence with its use of ingredients like Campari, Fernet, and Chartreuse Jaune (Yellow Chartreuse). There are less than twenty tables and just a handful of seats at the bar. Surprisingly, the most popular drink is their Espresso Martini.

One fun story: there is a portrait of a young boy near the *salle de bain* (bathroom) wearing a white shirt with a flipped-up collar and a velvet jacket. The staff refers to him as Young Chuck, and he is their resident ghost. To keep him calm, they give him a lil taste of Green

Chartreuse every night before locking the door. The one night they didn't, the general manager told us, and the next day almost everything went wrong. Glasses were constantly breaking, a staff member fractured a finger while carrying a heavy tray, and the ice machine short circuited.

So, cheers to Young Chuck and this eclectic Parisian-inspired sanctuary that is always on our go-to list.

NEW ORLEANS SOCIAL HOUSE

752 Tchoupitoulas Street
New Orleans, LA 70130

We call it NOSH, and it's a great meetup spot mainly because of its social hour specials, ridiculous wine list, and, of course, bubbles. The thing is, you can be casual, romantic, or just all out festive to enter here; the only requirement is to be social! There is a TV with rotating pics of guests taken from the digital ring light camera setup. So many smiling faces and fist pumps and kissy faces on the big screen. There's a hot pink bathtub for amazing selfies and several sexy seating areas for groups of five or six. The long bar seats a little more than a dozen people. Everything is eclectic and colorful. The art is so fun and inspires new-world glam. A killer sound system has all the songs we love with just enough bass. It is really busy on the weekends, be warned.

The cocktail menu has a flurry of the classics mixed with some fun original options like the Limoncello Spritzer and Smoked Grapefruit with Monkey Shoulder Scotch and Campari. Yum! Fun has been served up here since 2017. It's a great place to have a drink or two before going to its sister restaurant, which is connected by a glass door, Tommy's Cuisine, best known for its Italian-Creole food and extensive wine selection.

SMOKED GRAPEFRUIT

¾ oz. Monkey Shoulder Blended Malt Scotch Whisky

½ oz. Campari

¼ oz. Cocchi Americano

½ oz. fresh lemon juice

½ oz. simple syrup

1 oz. Laphroaig Single Malt Scotch Whisky

1 orange twist, to garnish

1. Combine all of the ingredients, except the Laphroaig and orange twist, in a cocktail shaker with ice. Shake 10 to 15 times, and strain into a coupe.

2. Float the Laphroaig on top. Express the orange twist and garnish.

THE PEACOCK ROOM

501 Tchoupitoulas Street
New Orleans, LA 70130

The first time I came here, years ago, all I could do was peruse the décor in awe—deep turquoise walls, funky chandeliers, and a peacock theme. There is something to be said for walking into a place and suddenly having the urge to shake a tail feather. One might call it eclectic, as there are peacocks everywhere, including on the wallpaper. There are flamboyant decorative fake peacocks in all corners of the room; makes me wonder how many selfies people have taken with them. The space is divided; one side is more lounge-like, with a gold ceiling, the other has for seated cafe-style dining. No matter where you sit, you're sure to be captivated by the blue, green, and gold palette.

Once you get through all of that, it's easy to settle in and get in on what else happens here. On the last Friday of every month, you can come with your best headpiece or feather boa and get a free glass of champagne—so fun! Weekends offer a Birds of a Feather Brunch Together experience, and every Thursday there is live music, showcasing a local singer: a songbird.

Order a cocktail from the Pride of the Flock list, and it's guaranteed to come appropriately garnished and balanced. They use a great mix of sweet, smoky, and/or floral components to add just enough "fancy" to the drinks. Bartender Ellie boasts the Layover in Glasgow cocktail, inspired by the Paper Plane classic cocktail, which originated in Chicago in 2007. Ellie says her regulars come in droves in part because they like to show off the bar to their out-of-town friends. You are likely to see groups of ten here, especially for a girls' night out. Be sure to call ahead, as it's likely to be busy on any given night.

LOA BAR

221 Camp Street
New Orleans, LA 70130

We feel like we are floating into a haven where spirits are all around us...emphasis on "spirits." Loa are spirits of the Afro-Haitian Voodoo faith. Loa is also one of—if not the first—craft cocktail bar to enter the movement some twenty-five years ago in New Orleans . It's hard not to dive into the menu right away. Bedazzled as we are by the unique spirits and skill of the bartenders, we still frolic in the lobby, which is laid out as a mini museum with amazing artifacts, poignant art, and a back room that features different artists.

For many years we've gathered here mainly to take in what is a sweet taste of decadence both in liquid and physical form. The room is set up with separate seating areas, each with velvet upholstered couches, candles, amber glowing dangling lights, and round marble-top tables. This is the team that served us seasonal fancy drinks long before we realized how special craft spirits are. That is just one of many magnetic things to love here.

The menu hints of inspiration from France, Spain, Italy, Cuba, Africa, and the Caribbean...in essence, what New Orleans is made of. Each sip brings you closer to New Orleans: its seductive side, its historic side, its cultural side, its most beautiful side. After all, what is the most special feeling of all? Raising a glass with your nearest and dearest at a bar that pours art into a glass—now, that is spirit-sational!

SAZERAC BAR

130 Roosevelt Way (in the Roosevelt Hotel)
New Orleans, LA 70130

Your city may be represented by a flag or a bird, but in New Orleans we have an official cocktail: the Sazerac, which has been around since the mid-1800s.

Sazerac Bar holds true to the tradition of this drink with its mid-century African walnut panel walls, ornate mirrors, brass rail footstool, long mahogany bar (you can still see cigarette burns from the 1930s in the wood), oversized murals showing the diversity of our community, and bartenders decked out in sharp white jackets and black ties. It reminds you of a back-in-the-day bar with highbrow cocktails. A lot of visitors come through mainly because it's inside the famed Roosevelt Hotel and carries a long and strong history.

Fun fact: post Prohibition, women in NOLA couldn't drink in many places; they were only allowed in the Sazerac Bar on Mardi Gras Day. Of course, our lovely ladies were tired of the boys-only clubs and in 1949, in protest, they donned their best dresses and hats and "stormed the Sazerac," demanding to drink with the men. And just like that, women took a seat at the bar, and gone were the days of masculine sanctuary.

Another fun fact: the legendary senator/presidential candidate/governor Huey P. Long hung out here and was known for his love of the Ramos Gin Fizz. It's rumored

that a bullet hole in the wall was the result of a failed attempt to assassinate him. But the truth came out many years later that it was shot from a revolver that fell from the pocket of a drunk patron. We tell both versions of the story for fun.

SAZERAC

¼ oz. Herbsaint

1 sugar cube

1 dash water

3 dashes Peychaud's Bitters

1 ½ oz. Sazerac Straight Rye Whiskey

Lemon peel, to garnish

1. Rinse a chilled rocks glass with Herbsaint, discarding any excess, and set aside.

2. In a mixing glass, muddle the sugar cube, water, and bitters. Add the rye, fill the glass with ice, and stir until well chilled. Strain into the prepared glass.

3. Twist the lemon peel over the drink's surface to express the peel's oils, then garnish with the peel.

COPPER VINE WINE PUB

1001 Poydras Street
New Orleans, LA 70112

Prominently sitting on a busy downtown corner lot is a mini mecca for wine lovers. The Cooper Vine Wine Pub touts dozens of wines and eight local beers on tap. You kind of get the feeling of being in a little winery. The bar lives in a building built in the 1800s that was once owned by the Maylie family, who opened it as a family-

style dining restaurant. Now, many, many years later, it has morphed into a hip, funky wine bar.

Back in its restaurant days a famous bartender created The Roffignac, a cocktail named after Count Louis Philippe Joseph de Roffignac, who was New Orleans' tenth mayor from 1820 to 1828. The recipes may vary, depending on who you talk to, but usually this house special is made with grenadine, brandy, rye whiskey, and a lemon twist. You won't find it on many menus around town. It sort of lost popularity after Maylie's closed in 1986 after 110 years of service, but Copper Vine has it and proudly celebrates the history behind it.

You can lose yourself in the lush patio, which is over-flowing with greenery, tropical plants, and pretty flowers. It's a good choice if you're going to events at the nearby theaters, the Superdome, or the Arena.

We love their exclusive wine selection and have fun creating our own flights. The list changes seasonally with sommelier-selected wines that are picked based on quality and style. You can also join their wine club, which is always a blast.

GENTLE SAGE

1 ½ oz. Gentle Gin

¾ oz. white grapefruit juice

½ oz. agave nectar

¼ oz. fresh lemon juice

2 dashes Peychaud's Bitters

Fresh sage leaf, to garnish

1. Put all the ingredients, except the sage, in a cocktail shaker with ice and shake to blend. Pour through a strainer into a coupe glass.

2. Slap the sage leaf and use it to garnish.

COMPÈRE LAPIN

535 Tchoupitoulas Street
New Orleans, LA 70130

A popular bar for folks who work nearby or are meeting their sweetie at day's end. Grabbing a seat at the bar is the luck of the draw, as there are only a dozen or so stools. Cocktails here are inspired by the city and, of course, the classics.

Funny little story: one of the signature cocktails is called the Penny Bunny. It's served in a copper bunny rabbit vessel that holds forty ounces and weighs about four pounds. Over the years it became a fun fad to drink from the bunny and take pics. Sadly, it now appears the bunny may be doing its last hop. Enthusiasts have been taking the experience too far by stealing the bunnies and bragging about it on social media. Co-owner Larry Miller says he's shocked this is happening and has shamed people into bringing them back—he's even used a lil detective work (through names on reservations) to track people down and publicly reveal their sticky fingers. Anyhow, the bunnies aren't cheap, upwards of $400 each. The bar started with fifteen and is now down to five…and holding onto those for dear life.

According to their website, *compère lapin* is French for "brother rabbit" but it also refers to a Creole folktale featuring a mischievous bunny. The irony here is knee slapping. A place named after a trickster rabbit is now finding itself being tricked out of their copper bunny drinking vessels. During our visit, no bunnies hopped away, but we supported their efforts to get their bunnies back.

Larry Miller and chef/co-owner Nina Compton moved to New Orleans from Miami and intentionally opened Compère Lapin in June, mainly because few people visit New Orleans in the dead of summer and that forced them to get to know the locals and make friends.

Chef Nina, who is from St. Lucia, was featured on Bravo's *Top Chef* season 11, and is a James Beard Award winner. It's important to her and Larry that their bar has the same high standards as the restaurant. As a result, there has been a stellar lineup of bartenders working with Chef Nina to create drinks to complement the food, as well as to assemble a super solid wine list. Larry told us the bar is a major extension of the restaurant because they are constantly trying to come up with fun new and unique flavors.

LUCY'S RETIRED SURFERS BAR & RESTAURANT

701 Tchoupitoulas Street
New Orleans, LA 70130

A party atmosphere to be sure since 1992. Be warned, the drinks pack a powerful punch. Belly up to this bar and ask for the popular Shark Attack. It's made with three different spirits (vodka, rum, and gin) and is sure to knock any mermaid off its tail. Other fun drinks are the Scorpion Shot (if sting is your thing) and the island-inspired Rum Rickey. There are plenty of Margaritas, frozen drinks, and themed shots. This isn't for the faint of heart.

Located in the Warehouse District, it isn't far from heavily-populated attractions, which makes it perfect for those who live, work, and play nearby. It's totally laid-back and mostly busy for basketball and football games, conventions, or any reason to kick it. Many of us meet up after work for a quick chat and libation. This definitely isn't your typical cookie-cutter bar. The super-fun theme gives a nod to retired surfers around the globe. Come here to have a wild time and enjoy the "hang ten" surfboard decorations and high energy. All you have to do it show up and let the fun begin. Oh, and you can bring your dog.

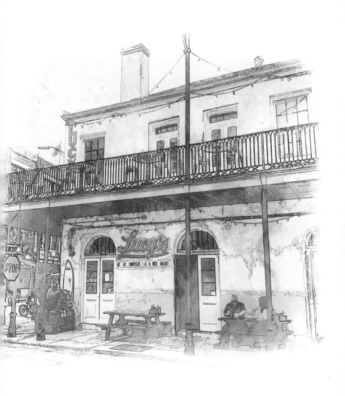

More Downtown and Central Business District Favorites

PLUCK
722 Girod Street

Whether you're new to the game or not, this place makes it easy to fall in love with vino. Great snack pairings too.

DOUBLE DEALER
129 Roosevelt Way

A speakeasy with live shows tucked away under the historic Orpheum Theater. Everything you would imagine: feathers, velvet seating, and vintage cocktails.

THE POLO CLUB LOUNGE
300 Gravier Street (inside Windsor Court Hotel)

Feels like a sexy, swanky English night club with live singers, comfy leather furniture, and good cocktails.

BARONESS ON BARONNE
339 Baronne Street

We, the authors, own this bar. It used to be a Quiznos that Ellen Degeneres donated to a local entrepreneur after Hurricane Katrina. After that, we snagged it in 2010. We've sold the most Chartreuse cocktails in the country for many years running, mainly for spirit education. Located in the heart of NOLA, we are sophisticated yet relaxed.

Favorite Rooftop Bars

ODD BIRDS NOLA
914 Union Street (inside Selina Catahoula Hotel)

THE POOL CLUB
550 Baronne Street (inside Virgin Hotel)

ABOVE THE GRID
317 Baronne Street (inside NOPSI Hotel)

ALTO
600 Carondelet Street (inside Ace Hotel)

INGENUE
1111 Gravier Street (inside Troubadour Hotel)

ROSIE'S ON THE ROOF
1000 Magazine Street (inside Higgins Hotel)

VUE ROOFTOP BAR
1600 Canal Street (inside Ponchartrain Hotel)

GARDEN DISTRICT

A family-friendly neighborhood close to a street car that travels along boulevards lined with opulent mansions, upscale restaurants, trendy bars, and historic landmarks. In the 1800s the land was sold to well-off Americans who did not want to live with Creoles in the French Quarter.

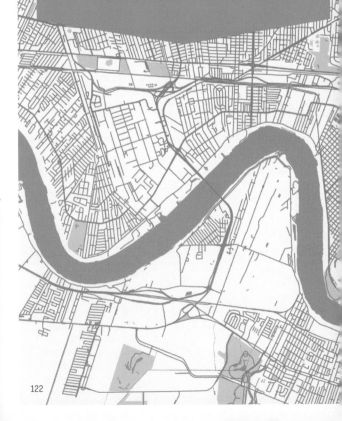

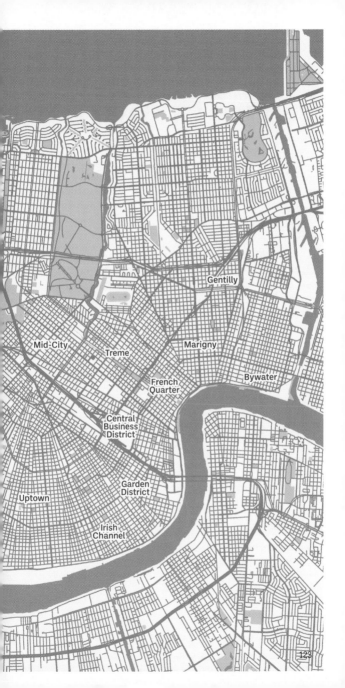

Mid-City

Treme

Gentilly

Marigny

Bywater

French
Quarter

Central
Business
District

Garden
District

Uptown

Irish
Channel

BARREL PROOF

1201 Magazine Street
New Orleans, LA 70130

A dark neighborhood dive bar at first glance, but once your eyes adjust to the darkness, take a closer look and you'll find more than 350 whiskeys and craft beers from all over the world. No matter your hankering, they are sure to carry your spirit of choice. Not sure what to drink? The bartenders will happily talk you through the long list. Happy hour is every day and offers $6 Old Fashioneds and mini frozen margs. Friday nights are standing room only, so pack your patience.

I used to come here when it was the beloved dog-loving Bridge Lounge and admittedly didn't know what to expect once the new owners took over. But the renovations don't disappoint, and it's obvious by the design that they love the space too. The rustic ceilings are low, hardly any windows, tin and wood walls and hardly any windows, and it always feels like there is a party going on.

In December this place looks like a holiday explosion, with upside-down trees, tinsel, lights, and ornaments that transform the bar into a wonderland of Christmas cocktails. They call this "Miracle" (the idea originated in New York) and it now can be found in bars in dozens of cities across the country, encouraging outta-this-world decorations and festive drinks during the holidays.

Grab a Sharpie or a piece of chalk if you're headed to the restroom, and join in on the ongoing graffiti and sticker collage. And if all of the whiskey gives you the munchies, there is a small kitchen; try the brick oven pizza. There is ample outdoor seating.

THE RUSTY NAIL

1100 Constance Street
New Orleans, LA 70130

I smile every time I see it. The bartender wears a shirt with a famous quote from Tennessee Williams: "America has only three cities: New York, San Francisco, and New Orleans. Everywhere else is just Cleveland." We could not agree more. The crowd is all over the place, from college students to millennials to the over-sixty crowd; they all come to the Nail in droves. The bar is dark, rustic, and worn; the patio has a totally different ambiance. It's surrounded by tall bamboo, palm trees, and hanging ferns, with accent lighting all around.

It's easy to get lost in the comfort and conviviality here. People come in workout clothes, business suits, and everything in between. The bartenders know 70 percent of the clientele by name. A lot of experienced bartenders work here. It's not just beer and mixed drinks; there is an extensive spirits selection, particularly whiskey, with more than sixty bourbons and dozens of Scotches from around the world to choose from. If you're undecided, there is a list of staff picks.

It's called The Rusty Nail because it was a favorite drink of one of the owners' fathers. It's a stiff one that became popular in New Orleans in the 1960s.

THE RUSTY NAIL

2 oz. Scotch

¾ oz. Drambuie

1 dash Angostura Bitters

Lemon twist

1. Stir all ingredients, except the lemon twist, in a mixing glass with ice to dilute, and serve on the rocks.

2. Express lemon and discard

THE AVENUE PUB

1732 St. Charles Avenue
New Orleans, LA 70130

Have you ever felt so strongly about something that you'd protest, write letters, or boycott if it went away? Something like that happened here. Avenue Pub has been on St. Charles Avenue for as long as I can remember (shhh, but I think I had my first beer here when I was in high school). It was popular before we knew what a microbrew was. The shabby building sat quietly on the avenue and was the place to go for beer lovers, but over time it strayed from the beer and developed more of a restaurant vibe. The regulars were having none of it, got serious, and gave warning—bring the local brews back or else. They wanted their beer bar back! The building went on the market for $1.5 million, and fifteen minutes later it sold.

Local industry folks joined forces to buy it and quickly revamped the décor and menu to make it a down-home beer pub again. One customer brought back ten people, who brought back another ten, who brought back ten, and so on...and here we are now.

Now there are forty-two beers on tap, mostly local brews plus some Germans and Belgians. The food menu is modest. Tiffany lamps hang, a motorized train traces the perimeter of the first floor, and there is a pennant salute to our two favorite teams: LSU and the Saints.

There's a backyard patio with old school ashtrays. The pub is not open 24-7 like it used to be, but it will stay open late and open early for special occasions.

DELACHAISE WINE BAR & BISTRO

3442 St. Charles Avenue
New Orleans, LA 70115

Ask your friends, "Where should we go tonight?" and they are likely to top the list with Delachaise. Duh. Because, to many of us, it's the quintessential local joint, not pretentious, a no-brainer decision and a place that doesn't take itself seriously for a wine bar. The bartender is likely to sit at your table for a quick chat while rattling off the latest wines the bar has to offer. It's a great place for date night, people watching, and getting mesmerized by the sound of streetcars rolling along historic St. Charles Avenue. Romantic indeed, with a cute lil courtyard, mahogany red walls, and comfy seating.

I talked to a bartender there who said, "Every day I come to work, someone I know comes in for a drink" It's the kind of place where one drink becomes three and, next thing you know, you've made friends with people around the bar. Yes, there's carefully selected top-shelf liquor, but there are more than 300 wines and a few frozen drinks. Definitely a *Cheers* kinda vibe.

I'm willing to bet that if you ask someone who lives here where to go for a great drink, they would point you in this direction. Definitely take them up on it; we'll be waiting on ya.

THE COLUMNS

3811 St. Charles Avenue
New Orleans, LA 70115

Close your eyes and imagine a late 1800s style Italianate mansion. Inside The Columns the bar mimics your wildest thoughts. We walk through twelve-foot-high doors past deep, dark wood paneling, fluted columns, wood-paneled ceilings, and giant elegant crystal chandeliers with a few modern twists thrown in. It oozes Southern charm. For us, it's a meeting place for friends and has been for many years, for happy hours, for weddings, and more. It's also been used as a movie set. You can also enjoy drinks on the second-floor balcony or on the front porch and watch the streetcar pass by on what locals call "the Neutral Ground," historically the land that divides opposing lanes of traffic and also the place where we watch Carnival parades and catch the streetcar (everywhere else, it's called a "median").

There are so many reasons to love the The Columns: the history, the scenery, its relics (including the original mahogany staircase), the rumored friendly ghosts who live here, the massive front porch lined with 100-year-old oak trees, some of which have Mardi Gras beads dangling on them year-round. No matter how you're dressed, somehow you feel fancy, in a low-key way.

Sitting here makes me think back to the original owner, a tobacco mogul. The amount of passion he put into the details speaks loudly. We are thankful that no matter how many times it's been renovated over the years, many of the original pieces are still at The Columns. This is a true New Orleans hangout spot with cocktails that are solidly made and served creatively. But don't be surprised if you find yourself equally mesmerized by the atmosphere.

THE COLUMNS MARTINI

1 oz. Hendrick's Gin

1 oz. Grey Goose Vodka

¾ oz. Le Quintyne Blanc Royal Vermouth

¼ oz. olive brine

Olive, to garnish

Lemon twist, to garnish

1. Combine all of the ingredients in a mixing glass with a few ice cubes, stir well, and strain into a chilled cocktail glass.

2. Garnish with olive and lemon twist.

HOT TIN

2031 St. Charles Avenue
(in the Pontchartrain Hotel)
New Orleans, LA 70130

Only one of the two elevators takes you up to this eleventh-floor bar—you can't miss it. It's trimmed in gold and labeled *Hot Tin PH*; it's not uncommon to be crammed in with several people anxious to get there. The doors open, and you are immediately face-to-face with a magnificent 270-degree view of the city, with an open-air terrace and enclosed penthouse lounge. It reminds you of a *Sex in the City* night or a VIP after-party complete with trendy music, heads bobbing, and lots of laughter. This is selfie central. I'll be willing to bet no one leaves here without popping off a pic or two. It's the kind of vibe that makes you want to let people know you were chilling on this rooftop.

Every corner of the room has a different theme, from Caribbean to Old New Orleans, from eclectic knick-knacks to classic statues. If you can't find something to talk about here, you're simply not trying. It's plenty chic, and it gives even the most seasoned New Orleanian pause. And let us not forget the impressive cocktail lineup and humble mixologists. Don't see anything that tickles your fancy on the menu? Not to worry, just tell the bartender what you like, and they'll mix up something hot.

RITA HAYWORTH

1 ½ oz. tequila blanco

¾ oz. apricot liqueur

¾ oz. lime juice

1 ¼ oz. Chipotle Agave (blend chipotle paste with agave)

1. Combine all of the ingredients in a shaker tin with ice, shake well, and strain into rocks glass. Salt the rim of glass, if desired.

TRACEY'S ORIGINAL IRISH CHANNEL BAR

2604 Magazine Street
New Orleans, LA 70130

Drink, eat, and swag, ya heard? That's what Tracey's wants us to do, and we are here for it. It's hard not to notice the hundreds of parasols hanging upside down from the ceiling, made by their regular customers. This bar has nailed the concept of being part of the community, which it has been since 1949.

Back then, they were the first to have air-conditioning, color TV, and frosted mugs, so you can imagine how popular they were. It was a great way for hard-working Irish dockworkers to reward themselves at the end of the day.

Not much has changed over the years. People still gather here for same comforts. They went from bragging about being the first to have color TV to now having twenty-two TVs that play the Saints, Pelicans, LSU, and Tulane games. We are a party town, and this is a great place to do it. It's laid-back and casual, the kind of bar where you can hang out for hours, especially if you catch a day when crawfish is being served.

What's better than being in the best city in the world, sipping on a Guinness and claiming the luck of the Irish?

THE RUM HOUSE

3128 Magazine Street
New Orleans, LA 70115

The doors opened in 2009 and since then, the Rum House has had a chilled-out Caribbean vibe, where everyone is *irie, mon.* The colorful oversized Bob Marley mural has him staring you in the eyes and making you wish you were on the beach with a Piña Colada swaying to the rhythmic sounds of island jams, making a memory to live into infinity. Instead, you're in NOLA, where the laid-back attitude also works, since we've often been described as "the northernmost Caribbean city."

The Rum House was one of the first places with outdoor seating that I can remember. It's casual, with food served on tin plates, water in mason jars, and seating mostly at picnic benches. The rum drinks are served in Hurricane glasses. It's always busy and loud, but not from the reggae music, which plays softly in the background. It's from the many conversations happening all around you.

The biggest day of the year at the Rum House is St. Patrick's Day because the parade passes right in front. They're open 362 days of the year.

At other bars, we find there are many tropical drinks with big names and complicated recipes, but here the menu is relaxed, funky, and easy-going. They have 200 rums from all over the world, and most of the syrups and mixes are made in-house and apparently top secret. Locals kept business alive during the pandemic and, by the look of things, they continue to drop in.

THE BOWER BAR

1320 Magazine Street
New Orleans, LA 70130

If there were ever a time to slow down and smell the roses, this would be it. A tranquil bar with outdoor seating in the historic Lower Garden District neighborhood, The Bower Bar feels like a meditation garden or a calm retreat. The interior of the bar is a thing of beauty. The ceiling is alive with hanging plants and twinkling string lights; a small atrium is in the middle of the room. Everything here is soft, right down to the lighting, seating, and muted tones. This modern building is a standout along this centuries-old street.

During the pandemic, this was a place of comfort; it became a go-to place for folks to get out and socialize. In 2020 few bars in New Orleans had outdoor seating, so people came in droves for fellowship and to drink and be safe in the open air. The momentum never left. The cocktails are outrageously creative, and the bartenders will tell you the story behind each one. The drinks have seasonal ingredients, and recipes rotate accordingly. For larger groups, ask to sit in the comfy alcoves and close the curtains for a bit of privacy.

STORYVILLE MAI TAI

1 ½ oz. spiced rum

½ oz. orgeat syrup

½ oz. fresh lime juice

½ oz. grapefruit juice

2 dashes Angostura Bitters

Edible glitter (preferably maple), for rimming

Fresh mint sprig, to garnish

1. Combine all of the ingredients, except glitter and mint, in a cocktail shaker with ice, shake well, and strain into a coupe glass.

2. Garnish with mint and edible glitter.

PARADISE LOUNGE

1507 Magazine Street
(inside the Hotel Saint Vincent)
New Orleans, LA 70130

Talk about a storied past. This red brick building dates back to 1861, when it was the Saint Vincent's Infant Asylum. The entryway, foyer stairwell, balconies, and patios are grand. This may sound a bit spooky, but actually it's a lovely story. A woman named Margaret Haughery, an Irish immigrant (and orphan), was beloved in New Orleans as a philanthropist. She opened Saint Vincent's as a refuge for unwanted and sick children of all races. Back then, yellow fever was running rampant. I have a friend who was adopted from here fifty years ago and she has a sweet, emotional reaction every time she comes for drinks.

Saint Vincent's was brought back to life after years of being many things, including a cheap, shabby hostel. Now it houses charming guest rooms, a restaurant, and three bars. A lot of the original features still stand, including the iron columns, some of the tile floors, and the doors and windows.

The bar menu in Paradise Lounge is modest but packs a powerful punch, with several handcrafted cocktails to choose from. Many of the drinks mix Italian and Creole flavors.

The first floor Chapel Club is for guests only—it hints at mischief, as there is no shortage of eclectic nude sketches strewn about. There is also a poolside bar. And there are ghost stories, to be sure—the sound of children laughing and playing, and a man who trolls the Chapel Bar and taps people on the shoulder while they use the bathrooms.

It's fun to soak up the history here while sipping. If maintaining Margaret's mission of integrity and humanity was part of the plan, the job was well done. The bars here welcome neighbors and visitors—of all kinds.

THE SAINT BAR & LOUNGE

961 St. Mary Street
New Orleans, LA 70130

The sign out front says "Cold beer, mixed drinks, free jukebox and good times." Reminds me of a grungy dungeon. It's mostly a late-night party spot and by "late-night" we mean the crowds don't really start coming until after 1 a.m. and stay until the wee hours of the morning, especially on the weekends. You go through two heavy black doors to get in, and then the entry way opens onto low ceilings, black spray-painted walls, and most everything is full of graffiti, including the cigarette machine and the TV screens. The place is filled with trinkets collected over the years, including moose heads, Christmas tinsel, bobbleheads, ceramic figurines, and a skull-shaped disco ball that hangs above the dance floor.

This is where you'll find locals, specifically service industry folks. The crowds pour in for karaoke and tiki once a week; there is a DJ on the weekends (don't even think about requesting a song). Drinks come in plastic cups, and the prices match the presentation. I'd stick with shots, beer, or regular drinks.

The wall near the bar is a mural of pics from the photo booth. I wonder if any of those folks remember taking a photo, much less putting it on the wall. There is a caged-in shrine in the middle of the room that holds old liquor bottles, mannequins, a guitar, and dusty candles honoring saints. Oh, and there is a claw machine that, for one dollar, will let you try your hand at grabbing a sex toy or a pack of smokes.

Back in the 1980s the bar was an Irish pub and got the nickname "the headless hooker bar" because a twenty-six-year-old barmaid was decapitated in the upstairs apartment. It was later sold and has been The Saint for years.

The Saint is open until 4 a.m. or later, depending on how late the crowds wanna roll.

THE TELL ME BAR

1235 St. Thomas Street
New Orleans, LA 70130

Driving to the bar had us questioning our GPS; going left, right, down a windy gravel road, only to open into a cute natural wine bar that unexpectedly sits under the Highway 90 bridge. This unique location, run by a couple of wine experts, is a hidden gem in the Lower Garden District.

The vibe makes you feel like you're ready to jump into the wine list feet first. We were intrigued by the lush greenery, fancy floors, fresh red roses, amazing artistic murals, sexy seating areas, and relaxed outdoor seating. It's great for a laid-back date night. One painting perhaps holds the key to the name; it reads in part "Tell me the truth, tell me to buy water, tell me poetry, tell me you love me, tell me freely, tell me more while saying less, tell me you love me again."

While the bar is new to the neighborhood, the team's experience is not. They are experts in natural and global wines and are happy to share their passion and skill with you. The bar has food pop-ups, a weekend DJ, and special wine events. Many call this bar NOLA's best kept secret, but I suspect it won't stay that way for long.

BAYOU BAR

2031 St. Charles Avenue
(in the Pontchartrain Hotel)
New Orleans, LA 70130

In its heyday, the bar inside the Pontchartrain Hotel was a warm den for celebrities like Frank Sinatra, Truman Capote, and Tennessee Williams (who worked on *A Streetcar Named Desire* while staying in a room upstairs). Celebrities came through mainly because things were kept private—secret. There were no mobile devices back then.

This is also where our beloved NFL franchise team The Saints was christened; the deal to create the team was signed here in 1967.

The bar is reminiscent of a lodge, tavern-like, with lots of wood, bird-themed wallpaper, swamp scenes, and comfy leather seating. When local bands are playing, it's hopping; the seating is limited, so come early and plan to stay late. There is a tiny dance floor if you're so inclined to shake a tail feather.

We love their happy hour and impressive whiskey and wine selections. Bayou Bar offers a party atmosphere that is a celebration of good drinks, old-fashioned thrills, and fine tunes.

Keep in mind, there are elegant guest rooms upstairs, if you drink too much.

More Garden District Favorites

HALF MOON BAR & GRILL
1125 St. Mary Street

A great neighborhood bar with games, a patio, well-priced stiff drinks, and a lot of funny patrons.

VERRET'S BAR AND LOUNGE
1738 Washington Avenue

Their motto: "Calm down, cool off, cocktails."

IGOR'S LOUNGE
2133 St. Charles Avenue

Nothing fancy, but open all day and all night—literally, it never closes. A place you can drink, grab a bite, and do your laundry while playing pool.

BALCONY BAR AND CAFE
3201 Magazine Street

The long wraparound balcony is great for late-night drinking and people watching. It's almost always packed with neighborhood folks. Stick with beer, shots, and simple drinks.

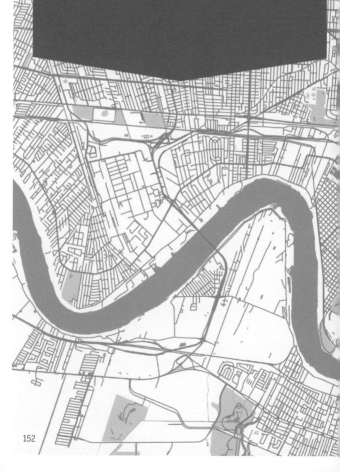

UPTOWN

A neighborhood where generations of families live. The streets are lined with beautiful old oak trees and nineteenth-century Victorian homes. The bars in this neighborhood are often packed but ooze laid-back Southern charm.

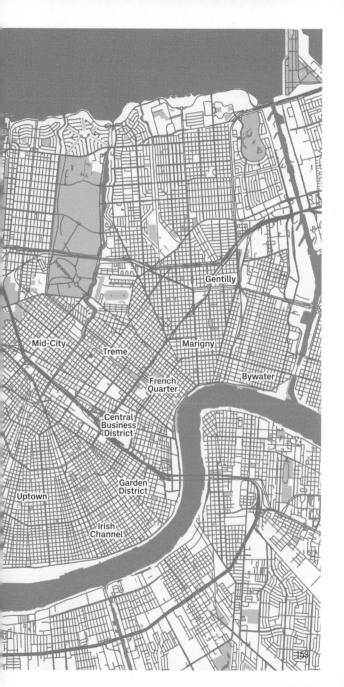

Mid-City

Treme

Gentilly

Marigny

Bywater

French
Quarter

Central
Business
District

Garden
District

Uptown

Irish
Channel

PORT ORLEANS BREWING CO.

4124 Tchoupitoulas Street
New Orleans, LA 70115

Their tagline, "Brewing Below Sea Level," is fitting since the city itself sits more than nine feet below sea level. Add to that, the brewery is positioned just across the tracks from the Port of New Orleans, on the East Riverside. Let's peel back the layers of the proverbial onion that is Port Orleans Brewing Co. to describe all the good that is here.

First, it's affiliated with two former Saints football players, offensive tackle Zach Strief (managing partner) and our local hero, safety Steve Gleason, who blocked a punt in the first game played in the Superdome after Hurricane Katrina, winning the game and giving all of us hope that we would return home. Gleason, who now has ALS, has an IPA named after him here, and a portion of the sales are donated to his foundation to help people living with the disease.

A glass wall separates pinball machines, comfy seating, and high-top tables from the rather large brewery. It runs with a thirty-barrel system and produces beer for 110 taps. There are seasonal selections and experimental beers, as well as Port Orleans' favorites, including Riverfront Lager, Vice Versa Hazy Juicy IPA, Riverfront Low Tide (a low-calorie lager), Bucktown

Brown Ale, Kennerbräu Kolsch, and Dorada (a Mexican-style lager).

Often we bring our dogs and settle in, outside or inside, depending on the unpredictable South Louisiana weather. Sid loves their beer, and I can never resist the taco stand and ice cream.

MILAN LOUNGE

1312 Milan Street
New Orleans, LA 70115

Walking in to Milan Lounge, you feel like you're entering your parents' unfinished basement, where no one is checking on you. One Wednesday night, a guy is screaming at Alexa to play Grateful Dead, another is asking for his doorbell back after lending it to the bar decades ago so the owner could keep the door locked late at night and the patrons safe. "That is," he says, "if you're not using it." A cast of characters, to be sure, and 95 percent are local. Most drinkers here live just blocks away and happily stumble home. The owner is no exception, one night saying goodnight to everyone at 10 p.m., throwing up his hand over his right shoulder, and mumbling, "Love y'all."

This bar is one of a kind, dating back to the 1930s. They say it used to be a gambling/bookie house back when people would come in on their way to work to place a bet, then return after work to grab a beer and see if they'd won.

This crew travels together, cooks meals for customers, and gives the food away—just because. They host the New Orleans Dart Club on Tuesdays, and perhaps the most impressive thing is that this bar throws potluck dinners to raise money for local charities. They've given away several hundred thousand dollars over the years.

They have two rules: no saving seats, and no crying at the bar. Ask for a receipt, and the bartender might laugh at you. A receipt? "Hey, Alexa, print a receipt," he chuckles. These are wholesome friendships here, which is why the owner turned the Milan Lounge into what he calls "the most trusted bar in the neighborhood."

HENRY'S UPTOWN BAR

5101 Magazine Street
New Orleans, LA 70115

Their slogan: "Serving beer since before you were born."

Henry's opened in the late nineteenth century and was said to have been a favorite drinking place for Lee Harvey Oswald, who notoriously assassinated President John F. Kennedy A bartender at the time said Oswald got kicked out once for handing out Communist brochures. Look beyond the bar, and there is a six-foot cardboard cutout of JFK leaning against the back wall—you can't miss it.

Sitting on the corner of this quiet Uptown neighborhood, Henry's is a longstanding watering hole (more than 100 years) that locals love to call "the home of cheap beers." While our city has plenty of shabby spots with cheap drinks, this is the one that is like a home away from home. It gets wild during Mardi Gras; this is one of the busiest corners on the parade route. On any given night, spirit-filled patrons like to karaoke their best renditions of their favorite songs, or take part in trivia games.

It's unlikely you'll find folks from other parts of town here; many travel just a few blocks to get here and happily stumble home. It's a neighborhood bar, and that's how we like it. We come here for friendly faces and the comforts of home, from the A/C window unit to the all-too-familiar repetitive conversations we often overhear.

Most municipalities don't allow bars to operate near schools, yet the all-girls Xavier Prep High School is directly across the street. How is that possible? Well, the bar was here first, so that is how they are able to stay—they're grandfathered in.

We order PBRs, sink into the worn barstools, and admire the wall scape. There is a Tulane University connection, so there are dozens of pictures of championship games, alumni, and autographs from players and coaches. If you are unfamiliar with the Tulane Green Wave before walking in, you just might become a Tulane University fan walking out.

BOULIGNY TAVERN

3641 Magazine Street
New Orleans, LA 70115

It's your neighborhood watering hole on steroids. Chic and modern with a twist of days of old. Dark wood paneling, dimly lit sconces, and a couch along the front bay window that looks like it came straight out of the 1970s.

You'll see everyone here, from your grandmother draped in diamonds and pearls, to young socialites, to dudes sporting jeans and sneakers. While we are waiting for our cocktails (fig-infused Old Fashioneds), our fries come. The lady sitting next to us, who looks like she finally got a mom's night out, excitedly leans over and asks to taste them. Of course, it's what we do in NOLA. We share drinks, stories of revelry, and, yes, food…it isn't uncommon to give away a bite or two. If she's happy, we are happy, the bar scene is happy, and all is well at the tavern.

But…ahh, the music! Would you believe they play old vinyl on an old school record player? And you can bring in your own albums to play, if you want. Intentionally, there are no TVs, which inspires conversation.

So, we ask the excited mom why she comes here. She tells us that she loves dive bars, but here the bartenders aim for cocktails with perfection, and no one here is a stranger...as life should be. Fries, anyone?

THE CHLOE

4125 St. Charles Avenue
New Orleans, LA 70115

In New Orleans, we like to party and gather on our front porches. It's where we let the good times roll, it's how we keep up with ya mom and 'dem. It's the place where we catch up with each other, eat, drink, and spend our summer and spring days. It is the epitome of Southern culture. But if you "get a wild hair," as we say in New Orleans, and want to hop over to another porch, The Chloe is a good choice, with its wrought-iron gates, grand patios, and front porch that dates back to the mid-1800s. Fire pits or slow-spinning fans are in use, depending on the season. Inside, the bar is eloquently evocative of a mid-nineteenth-century Victorian hotel. Most of the fine spirits are atop the fireplace, arranged altar-like. The happy hour is a real winner, offering $7 Daiquiris, Negronis, and Margaritas.

The atmosphere is everything that is Uptown NOLA, from well-appointed alligators and lizards, birds, and faux animals to lush greenery and egret murals. A local woodworker perfected the bar and its mahogany parlor-style setup. It's small but impressive, perfect for the rich Uptown neighborhood feel. The patio and a pool in the back also sport their own bar. Imagine taking in the scorching summer sun while sipping on your favorite libation. Ahh, heavenly!

The glamorous gals at the neighboring table squeal when describing the Espresso Martini here. (Side note: they're already on drink number three. Plus they say the heated pool is, in a word, awesome. We agree.)

Like many Uptown properties, this one has had many lives over the centuries (private residence, boarding-house, hotel). We applaud the fact that many original pieces were restored while others were updated. We love that we can walk in and fall into comfort that reminds us of Grandma and Grandpa's really cool, big-ass house.

CHLOE DANCER #2

1 oz. Bolden Four Count Vodka

½ oz. Mommenpop Kumquat-POP

½ oz. Nardini Acqua di Cedro Liqueur

½ oz. fresh lemon juice

3 oz. sparkling rosé, to top

1. Combine all of the ingredients, except the sparkling rosé , in a cocktail shaker with ice, shake well, and strain into a coupe glass.

2. Top with the sparkling rosé.

OAK

8118 Oak Street
New Orleans, LA 70118

If you love wine like I do, you've met your match here! Yes, you can come casual, but this place has a fancy flair. It's modern, and you'll find stylish patrons here. Not sure what to get? Not to worry, one of the team members will help you pair wine or drinks with any dish you choose.

Located in the Carrollton/Riverbend neighborhood, locals flock here for its extensive wine list, beer, and specialty spirits. It's literally just steps from the streetcar, so all you have to do is hop on and hop off for this go-to destination for good wine and great times. It lends itself to a fun start to the night, and it's also a nice place to grab and go if you're in the area. They made the décor so posh, light, and airy that most any angle is Instagrammable, and the bar itself is a show-stopper. The dozens of wine selections can be over-whelming...but just take a deep breath, ask a few questions, and jump in feet first. Also, check the schedule for live music.

MS. MAE'S

4336 Magazine Street
New Orleans, LA 70115

Don't worry about being late to this party, it's open twenty-four hours. This corner bar is full of cash-only, cheap drinks served in plastic cups. In addition to bar seating, there are booths, a few tables, and an outdoor patio with a big-screen TV for sports watching. It's definitely a hole in the wall, but we find ourselves here for a quick game of air hockey or pool just because it's a fun time. You'll always find groups of people loudly discussing what they did last night or what they are about to get into. Simply put, this is a favorite late-night or early-morning beer and shot watering hole and a treasure trove of blurry memories. You may be surprised to know there is a spike in customers from noon to 3 p.m. on any given day. The bartenders are beloved, and many have been here for years, so much so that we know them by name.

So, who is Ms. Mae? Her name was Florence Bingham, and she owned the joint from 1999 until 2010, when she sold it. Before that, she ran the place with ease, made her table rounds, and is responsible for the neighbor-hood vibe that has grown here over the years. She passed at age 83, but her memory lives with every drink poured.

Being here is like being in an old friend's basement; stickers litter the walls, and every framed picture tells a story. One reads "Pimps don't cry," another one says "I pooped today." This bar has seen its share of Mardi Gras parades and rowdy, loud, and large crowds. Be careful: if you stay too long and get trashed, you could end up on the Wall of Shame.

Some years back, siding was pulled off the building to uncover three sets of original gunstock doors hidden underneath. Now we can enter from the Napoleon Street side as well as from Magazine Street.

COOTER BROWN'S

509 S. Carrollton Avenue
New Orleans, LA 70118

Beer nerds to the back—that's where all the interesting stuff is—the internationals, stouts, seasonal IPAs, and dozens of rotating taps. It's not unusual for this place to be packed for sports, especially for the World Cup or any football game.

If you look up, there is a wall full of 100 statues of long-gone celebrities posing with different bottles of beer, everyone from Marilyn Monroe holding a Voluptuous Blonde Ale to Louis Armstrong, Joe DiMaggio, Babe Ruth, Ringo Star, and several former presidents. They call it a Beersoleum.

There are always a handful of neighborhood regulars holding court under one of the many huge TVs. Nowadays there are also groups sitting outside on the post-COVID patio. Don't expect table service; you have to go to any one of the three bars to order.

They've been serving here since 1977, so it's not unusual to see generations of folks coming through the doors. The beer selection has evolved as the bar has over the years, from corner bar to sports lover's destination. Alert: you may lose track of time eating oysters and throwing back beers because there are no windows.

And who is Cooter Brown? Well, if you're from the South, you've likely heard the phrase "drunk as Cooter Brown." He's the bar's mascot, depicted as a drunk man with a cowboy hat.

New Orleans Daiquiri Shops

When I think of the hottest days of summer, all I can think of is having a 44-ounce New Orleans–style 190 Octane Daiquiri.

Frozen Daiquiris are a staple, a summer must-have, something you'll see in most everyone's hand at least once in their life. We simply love them. We happily choose which high-proof spirit we want to mix it with, and then we take a leisurely stroll. These frozen drinks are favorites during Mardi Gras, festivals, and, hell, any given Sunday. We have ordered Daiquiris by the gallon to take to a crawfish boil, family gathering, or other social event.

Only In the Big Easy can you find a drive-thru Daiquiri shop. Yes, drive-thru, and it's 100 percent legal. In Louisiana we have an open container law, which means you can walk and sip, but the cup must be sealed with a lid and no straw protruding out the top. And no sipping while driving. So we get to our destination and sip the day, and sometimes the night, away.

More Uptown Favorites

CURE
4905 Freret Street

This upscale bar has nice elixirs, house-made syrups, and a roster of extreme bartending talent. One of the first places to crack the craft cocktail code years ago, which is why it was named one of America's best bars and is a James Beard Award winner.

MAPLE LEAF BAR
8316 Oak Street

Brass bands play from a cute little stage, and if you don't feel like dancing with the locals, there is a small patio for outdoor seating.

SNAKE AND JAKE'S CHRISTMAS CLUB
7612 Oak Street

As crazy as New Orleans is, this place takes the cake. This small, shabby lounge looks a little sketchy, but don't worry, it's all good. The inside is covered in red lights and esoteric vibes; the walls hold decades of secrets. The floors and tables are sticky. It's open every day, especially every Christmas.

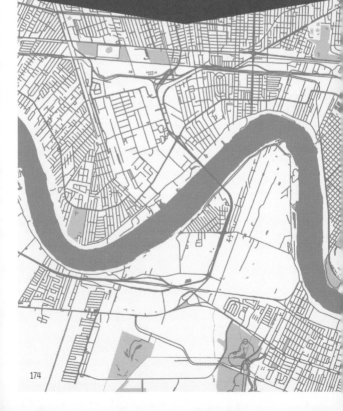

MID-CITY

Bars in this hip, diverse neighborhood are somewhat eclectic and are supported heavily by regulars and locals. The area is full of creative and artsy folks who love a good drink and good times at the many cocktail bars and outdoor wine and beer gardens.

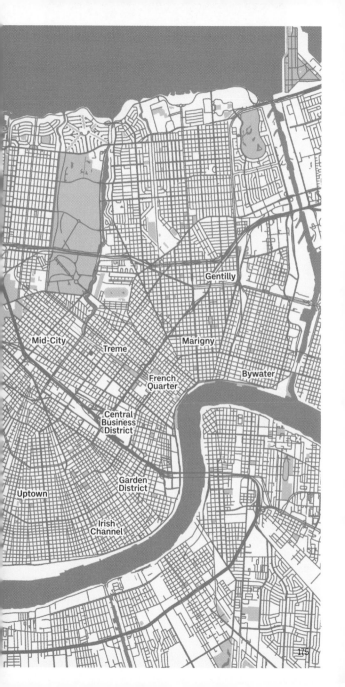

Mid-City

Treme

Gentilly

Marigny

French
Quarter

Bywater

Central
Business
District

Garden
District

Uptown

Irish
Channel

FINN MCCOOL'S IRISH PUB

3701 Banks Street
New Orleans, LA 70119

Looking for a pint, some small bites, and an authentic pub? This is a popular watering hole for Mid-City neighborhood folks. It actually got its name from folk singer Finn McCool. Speaking of music, the genre is never the same, but it's always rocking. Tonight it's Franky Beverly & Maze. Imagine the most iconic pub in Ireland married to a bar in New Orleans, and you get this happy place. I can't count the number of times I've spent St. Patrick's Day here; it is an all-out block party complete with Irish brews and tons of fun.

The menu has lots of Irish whiskey, Irish beer, and Irish coffee. Most folks come after work, so don't be surprised if you see your neighbors sipping a drink while rocking their baby before walking back home.

It's comfortable here, with six TV screens showing mostly sports, especially soccer; it's packed for football games. The decorations are mostly sports memorabilia: Saints' gear, rugby cleats, Irish-inspired posters, old stickers from the New Orleans 1984 World's Fair. Two sets of doors are wide open most of the time, and there's plenty of outdoor seating. There's a pool table in the middle of the room and usually always a line for it.

Perhaps most impressive is what this bar gives back to our community. They invite neighbors to shave their heads, with proceeds going to the St. Baldrick's Foundation, which raises money for childhood cancer research.

It's certainly not your average corner spot; it's a long-standing place that doesn't look like it's slowing down anytime soon.

BAYOU BEER GARDEN

326 N. Norman C. Francis Parkway
New Orleans, LA 70119

On any given day you will find the place packed wall to wall, standing room only. The lure here are the forty-five beers on tap, more than 200 different bottles and cans, plus the fact that it's connected to the court-yard of its sister bar, the Bayou Wine Garden.

Inside the modest shotgun double house, it's dimly lit, candles everywhere. Not surprisingly it's a beer drinker's paradise. It instantly reminds you of a familiar gathering where everyone's talking shit (fun stuff) while sipping everything from high-end $14 lagers and ales to $5 Heinekens to beers made with locally-grown hops. The list of brews is extensive and, quite frankly, impressive!

There is the huge outdoor patio, plenty of TVs for sports (especially our beloved Saints football team), and a wraparound zigzag bar. It's a social space that one bartender calls "the Swirl," a place where many different types of people connect and conversations begin to intertwine. Ask any brew-loving local about their favorite spots—this will most certainly top the list. Over the years we've watched it grow from a shabby pub to a renovated beer hub. People pop in from all over the world, my guess is because the hops are happening, the stouts are special, and the energy here is dope.

BAYOU WINE GARDEN

315 N. Rendon Street
New Orleans, LA 70119

Vino, anyone? My hand is raised! Let's head over to this chic little neighborhood wine garden in the Mid-City area. At first look the extensive menu could be intimidating, with forty-six wines on tap and hundreds more bottles from around the world. Of course, you can order a glass, bottle, or carafe.

The building is a New Orleans-style shotgun double, pristinely redone and redecorated with a wine-barrel-bottom bar and sexy lighting. It can get a bit crammed around the bar during the busiest hours, but it's all good because we are here for the same reason: the love of wine! Thank goodness it's casual, we can come as we are. #covidcute

The cheese pairings are appropriate, and the small bites complement the drink menu. A small list of craft cocktails is full of in-house recipes that include plum brandy, shochu, and fig-and-honey syrup. They have nailed what locals like to drink and eat. There's a little something special for just about everyone.

The team supports and plays host to community efforts like art markets and doggie adoptions. Looking through the wide-open French doors, there is outdoor seating with a lush garden, orchard stone, a four-tiered grand courtyard fountain, and dog bowls for our furry friends. There are TVs outside, but it seems this crowd may just glance up from time to time to check the score. The crowd is hipster, mature, trendy, and professional. You can choose to digitally order from the table to keep it simple or go to the walk-up bar, where there is a Frosé and Daiquiri machine. Add to all of this, the court-yard connects to its brother business, the Bayou Beer Garden. It's the most clever two-for-one in the city. Genius!

WRONG IRON ON THE GREENWAY

3532 Toulouse Street
New Orleans, LA 70119

The idea is to slow down, recharge, and have a good time with friends, hence the name "Wrong Iron." The name stems from the main railroad running in the opposite direction. So, while people are running home from work to do homework with children, you can decide to go the other way and head into the bar.

In 1894 Southern Railway used this route to allow trains to access nearby terminals. The owners of Wrong Iron kept the industrial vintage rail station theme and opened an outdoor-indoor playground for beer enthusiasts. So let's all stop, take a moment to grab a drink, and relax. The Lafitte Greenway is alongside the bar, and often you'll see bikers hopping off to break for a brew.

Outside is a large cozy patio with seating areas complete with fire pits, heaters, and blankets for the colder weather and large fans when it's crazy hot. We think this is a great idea, since the concept is giving life to an area that didn't really have much activity.

Inside is closed in with glass garage doors, brick walls, and one long-ass bar. Featured items include fifty draft beers, more than 100 different bottles, several wines (some on tap), six cocktails on tap, a full bar, New Orleans favorite summer Daiquiris, and even a few menu items from various pop-ups or food vendors. You can even get a wine tower for the table, which equals about two bottles of wine.

It's a great place to watch the game—there are big-screen TVs everywhere, twenty-eight to be exact. No need to worry about parking, whether you are biking or driving.

At the end of the day, Wrong Iron isn't fancy. It's simply a fun, large-scale beer garden.

NEYOW'S CREOLE CAFE

3332 Bienville Street
New Orleans, LA 70119

It's exciting to find a bar off the beaten path, one that is so popular that there is almost always a line circling the Mid-City block it sits on. If you miss the front door, don't worry—just look for the five-foot-tall gorilla out front that greets everyone who enters. The bar is modest and full of local brands. Signature drinks include two variations of rum punch (32 ounces).

Here's the thing about Neyow's: it takes us a while to get to the bar, mainly because as we go up the long staircase, we stop to chat with a friend we haven't seen in ages. Good luck passing the oyster grill, because it's likely to be surrounded by familiar faces asking, "How's ya mom and 'dem?" The owners hail from a long line of Creole families and have a huge following. The mural behind the bar highlights images only New Orleanians would understand, like a Hubig's Pie, a horse-drawn Roman Candy stand, culture-bearing Indians, colorful Creole cottages, second line umbrellas, and famous musicians.

Neyow's reputation has traveled by word of mouth into the ears of so many that visitors come in droves; there is a photo collage wall of all the celebs who have passed through. This is a family affair where everyone is welcome and, whether you're eating or drinking, you're guaranteed to leave satisfied.

BOW WOW FRUIT PUNCH

5 oz. silver rum

5 oz. gold rum

Sweet fruit punch

Maraschino cherry or orange or lime wedge, to garnish

1. Mix the silver and gold rums thoroughly in a tall glass filled with ice. Top with fruit punch.

2. Garnish with a cherry or orange or lime wedge.

VESSEL NOLA

3835 Iberville Street
New Orleans, LA 70119

Eat, drink, congregate…that pretty much sums it up. This former Lutheran church was thriving in the early 1900s. The original stained glass windows and Gothic design don't let you forget the building's religious beginnings. Where the pulpit once was, there is now a mural of cocktails. Seems like a simple thing, but there is beauty in the glassware; the team believes all great cocktails should be served in "proper vessels." (See what they did there? If the devil is in the details, Vessel nailed it. Even the ceiling mimics a ship's hull—another vessel.)

The bartender stops to tell many stories of the building being haunted, of exploding beer cans, strange sounds, unexplained shadows, employees saying they got the feeling of being pushed down the stairs. While she says she has never personally experienced any paranormal activity, she does hurry to get out quickly at the end of the night…just in case! (If you're curious, come see for yourself or check out *The Dead Files*, season 11, episode 7.)

This former church reinvented as a bar is now more of an art space, which is fitting, since many of us in New Orleans have no problem mixing creative pleasure and worship. It has fun local art, sexy lighting, long wooden tables in the center of the room, groovy music, and a bar to rival most any in town. High-end bottles sit on glass shelves, and at night the sconces and bookshelves glow red—spiritual symbolism? Either way, the copper pineapples strewn about welcome us...after all, what's New Orleans without a ghost story or two, right?

REVEL CAFE & BAR

133 N. Carrollton Avenue
New Orleans, LA 70119

This spot is run by an iconic couple, Chris and Laura McMillian. Chris is a longtime legend and pioneer in the cocktail world and has been a mentor to many bartenders along the way. He is a walking, talking book of knowledge on all things spirits and alcohol related. A national treasure, I'd say. Every time we chat, I leave the conversation with a sense of awe at what he knows and is happy to share with us youngsters.

You'll never get a sloppy or half-assed drink at this bar. Each one is masterfully done, sometimes by the legend himself. We see him a lot, tinkering around with syrups, aperitifs, and house made bitters.

This is not a grab-and-go place, mainly because you will be asking for a cocktail, then another, then, if you are lucky enough, Chris will sit down and tell you the latest fascinating thing his mind has dreamed up.

Revel has blue walls and a bi-level design. The menus, for both food and drink, are carefully curated. This gem is tucked away far from the tourist area, but it's worth the trip if you're in town.

SIDECAR

Sugar

1½ oz. cognac

¾ oz. orange liqueur (Cointreau is best)

¾ oz. fresh lemon juice

Orange twist, to garnish

1. Sugar the rim of a coupe glass, and set aside.

2. Add the cognac, orange liqueur, and lemon juice to a cocktail shaker and add ice. Shake until chilled. Strain into the glass.

3. Garnish with the orange twist.

THE BULLDOG

5135 Canal Boulevard
New Orleans, LA 70124

And

3236 Magazine Street
New Orleans, LA 70115

Talk about a double dose, there are two Bulldog locations. One of their claims to fame is having large, dog-friendly patios. Dogs are welcome inside too—they love dogs. Not surprisingly, there is a lot of canine-inspired art. And they are big on supporting local charities focused on animal-related causes.

Another great thing about the Bulldog is that their happy hour starts at 11:30 a.m. Yes, a.m. Cue the saying, "You can't drink all day if you don't start in the morning."

Every Thursday is locals' night, which is where you can find beer lovers crammed in to get a taste of some version of a gnarly barley for a special price. There are sixty-one taps that change a lot, so the selection is never quite the same.

Mid-City Bulldog is located at the end of the Canal Street streetcar line and near several cemeteries. Graveyard tours stop in for a brew at least three days a week. The bar is mostly decorated with wood and amber lighting. The couple next to us say, simply, "It's our bar."

The Uptown location is on busy Magazine Street and a great stop after a day of boutique or antique shopping. People just love to hang out here. It's easy to slide in and find yourself still here hours later.

CASK

5123 Canal Boulevard
New Orleans, LA 70124

Cask opened in 2018, shut down during COVID-19 in 2020, and reopened in March 2021. So, like many bars, it's had its share of ups and downs. The general manager says it's the local gatherings and big groups that really keep it going.

To keep many of us coming, there are lots of fun things to do, like trivia night, karaoke once a month, dance night with a local DJ, crawfish on Fridays during Lent, Tequila Tuesday with three different Margaritas for $5, and on Wednesday bottles of wine are half off. We also love '80s night.

The Canal Boulevardier and the Pomegranate Paloma are crowd favorites on the $12 specialty cocktails list. There is wine on tap, local brews, and a lot of parties here: weddings, corporate meetings, birthday celebrations, friendship networking, and Carnival gatherings.

Cask is modern, stylish, and chic, the interior done up in shades of blue with a great front patio. Walking in, you instantly feel relaxed. General manager Roxann is delightful and full of energy. Ask for her and tell her we sent you.

More Mid-City Favorites

TWELVE MILE LIMIT
500 Telemachus Street

The best cocktails in a dive bar. The name is an "unloved" or forgotten cocktail from the Prohibition era, and it's a good stiff one.

1 oz. silver rum
½ oz. rye whiskey
½ oz. cognac
½ oz. lemon juice
½ oz. grenadine

Put all ingredients in a cocktail shaker with ice. Shake to chill. Strain ingredients into a rocks glass, and garnish with a cherry or lemon twist.

DMAC'S
542 S. Norman Francis Parkway

A little bar with live bands and plenty of brews.

CHICKIE WAH WAH
2828 Canal Street

It's a little place but has big live bands performing jazz. A cute neighborhood joint that is always high energy.

SECOND LINE BREWING
433 N. Bernadotte Street

A fun place to sample great beer, though the wine selection is worthy as well. It's open seven days a week and is kid and pet friendly.

IRISH CHANNEL

This neighborhood dates back to the early 1800s, when, you guessed it, the first Irish families arrived. Today it's mainly residential, filled with working-class folks, fun restaurants, and a lot of breweries.

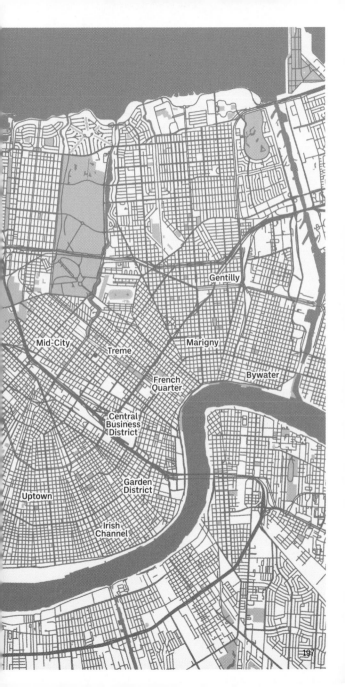

Gentilly

Mid-City

Treme

Marigny

Bywater

French
Quarter

Central
Business
District

Garden
District

Uptown

Irish
Channel

MIEL BREWERY & TAPROOM

406 Sixth Street
New Orleans, NY 70115

A perfect mix of food pop-ups, trivia night, frozen concoctions—along with the star of the show, the brew! The beer is made with local ingredients in the Irish Channel neighborhood brewery. There are about a dozen on tap, which are rotated out seasonally. Oh, the choices: hoppy IPAs, hazy hops, cream ales, lagers, and stouts.

It has a completely open-air patio with a long L-shaped bar, disco balls, and string lights. We saunter up and order today's featured cocktail, which happens to be the Michelada, made with pickle beer, lime, and tajin, topped with a tamarind straw (a sweet and sticky Mexican candy rolled in chili powder).

As we are about the leave, the trivia host asks, "Is the Portuguese man o' war a jellyfish?" Someone yells out "No!" the crowd loudly cheers, and they all toast each other. We dip out the side with a growler in one hand and our dogs in the other. We love that pets are welcome too.

PETE'S OUT IN THE COLD

701 Sixth Street
New Orleans, LA 70115

Every time we come, we have to wait to be buzzed in. Once eye contact is made with the bartender, she says, "It's just what we do." We share a laugh, and open a tab. "You wanna keep this bad boy open?" You bet we do.

This historic Irish Channel dive bar has been at this location since the 1800s. Back then, it was a bar, grocery store, hospital, and boardinghouse. Dockworkers came here to rest, drink, and frolic. Pete inherited the bar from his dad and officially opened it as Pete's Out in the Cold in the 1930s. There's really nothing of note in here: no art on the walls, no shelves filled with old trinkets collected over decades. The bar is done with expert millwork from back in the day and is original.

There is a small walk-up window that years ago was used to serve minorities and women, who weren't allowed inside. Man, I think to myself, if these walls could talk. Rumor has it that it sits on top of a cemetery, although we aren't exactly sure.

A Jack and Coke in a plastic cup slides across the bar in our direction, just six bucks. We don't tell a lot of people about Pete's because it's sort of a secret hideout for those "in the know."

OUT IN THE COLD

EST. 1931

PARASOL'S BAR & RESTAURANT

2533 Constance Street
New Orleans, LA 70130

This place has been in operation since 1952 when it was opened by Myrtle and Louis Passauer Jr. They named it after Louis Sr., whose nickname was "Parasol" because he always carried an umbrella. Also, they were convinced no one would be able to pronounce "Passauer." It was a clubhouse of sorts for neighborhood Irish folks and their favorite watering hole. But it wasn't all rainbows and unicorns; during segregation Black folks couldn't come in and were sold drinks through a small side window that still exists today.

Parasol's is the place to be during their huge St. Patrick's Day street party, which draws thousands of people every year. It takes months for the bar to prepare for the large crowds that dance and drink all day and into the night.

Television fame has shined a spotlight on Parasol's. Not only was it featured by Guy Fieri on the Food Network, it's in an episode of *The Simpsons*, when Homer is running around New Orleans eating food. If you haven't seen it, it is hilarious.

Sitting at the original bar, we can see cigarette burns in the wood from days of old. Imagine the conversations that have been had here! It goes without saying that this small neighborhood bar is open seven days a week. The most popular drink is a Boilermaker made with Miller High Life and Tullamore D.E.W. Triple Distilled Irish Whiskey; also, try the Frozen Irish Coffee.

The Irish flag waves around, we grab a bite and a brew, and promise to return soon.

Gentilly

This neighborhood is full of nineteenth-century shotgun homes and twentieth-century bungalows. It's known for being diverse and full of neighborhood watering holes and eclectic restaurants.

SKINNY & MARIE'S TAVERN
3831 Clematis Street

Known for the best ice-cold beer in the neighborhood, there are a few TVs, a few pool tables, and fun frozen drinks. Totally laid-back with lots of locals.

JOCKEY'S PUB AND SPORTS BAR
1841 Gentilly Boulevard

Get a beer and a shot for $6. They also offer good Margaritas and buckets of beer and Bloody Mary's. It's near the horse racing track. It's a fun little place to chill out, sit outside and maybe meet a new friend.

BROOKS SEAHORSE SALOON
1648 Gentilly Blvd

Known as the place to go before or after our famous Jazz Fest. They play blues or jazz music depending on the day, and there are alligators hanging on the walls. You can grab a shot, a beer, or a simple cocktail. This place is truly Nawlins!

About the Authors

Camille Whitworth is the co-owner and operator of the craft cocktail lounge Baroness on Baronne, which has been in New Orleans' downtown location for more than a decade. Baroness is the city's most eclectic and unique place for an array of small gourmet plates and an impeccably prepared cocktail. Whitworth is also the owner and operator of the New Orleans Drink Lab, an interactive cocktail venue where fun cocktail classes are taught and the venue serves as an incubator for bartenders. Whitworth also writes a cocktail blog, Drink Up Nola, for myneworleans.com.

Whitworth is also a professional journalist and the CEO of her media company, Media by Design, which specializes in public speaking, media consulting, commercial production, and media coaching. Whitworth worked for NBC affiliates for twenty-seven years and was the main anchor at WDSU New Orleans (NBC) for fourteen years.

Sidney Webb is the co-owner of Baroness on Baronne. Webb is proud to deliver the ultimate cocktail experience to locals and visitors. Inspired to infuse local products, flavors, and fun into cocktails, he follows a concept that brings drinking to a new level in the Crescent City and hopes to give guests an unforgettable experience. His mother, who has Caribbean roots, dabbled in the industry and instilled the value of creating a warm and inviting atmosphere where people could relax, drink, and enjoy themselves. Inspired by her legacy, he embarked on the journey to explore the diverse realms of spirits, ingredients, and mixology techniques.

Webb is also an actor and has been in many motion picture and television series, including *Claws*, *Leverage Redemption*, *Your Honor*, and *National Champions*.

About Cider Mill Press
Book Publishers

Good ideas ripen with time. From seed to harvest, Cider Mill Press strives to bring fine reading, information, and entertainment together between the covers of its creatively crafted books. Our Cider Mill bears fruit twice a year, publishing a new crop of titles each spring and fall.

"Where good books are ready for press"
501 Nelson Place
Nashville, Tennessee 37214

cidermillpress.com